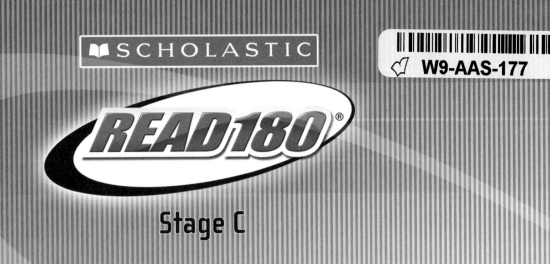

SCHOLASTIC

READ 180®

Stage C

Test-Taking Strategies

W9-AAS-177

Copyright © 2005, 2003, 2001 by Scholastic Inc.

All rights reserved.   Published by Scholastic Inc.   Printed in the U.S.A.

ISBN 0-439-67070-5

SCHOLASTIC, READ 180, rBOOK, SCHOLASTIC RED, SCHOLASTIC ACHIEVEMENT MANAGER, SCHOLASTIC READING INVENTORY, SCHOLASTIC READING COUNTS!, and associated logos and designs are trademarks and/or registered trademarks of Scholastic Inc. LEXILE and LEXILE FRAMEWORK are registered trademarks of MetaMetrics, Inc.

3 4 5 6 7 8 9 10   66   14 13 12 11 10 09 08 07 06 05

Contents

Introduction to Test-Taking Strategies 4

Overview of Resources 6

red Scholastic Red Professional Development:
Assessment Tests and the Struggling Reader 7

How to Help Students Prepare for Exit Exams 14

Reading Test Strategies: Lessons and Practice

Lesson 1: Making an Educated Guess 18

Lesson 2: Answering Fill-in-the-Blanks 21

Lesson 3: Restating the Question 24

Lesson 4: Previewing Questions 27

Lesson 5: Using Vocabulary Strategies 30

Lesson 6: Literal & Interpretive Questions 33

Lesson 7: Answering Proofreading Questions 36

Lesson 8: Using Cue Words: Compare, Cause/Effect 38

Lesson 9: Using Cue Words: Sequence, Fact/Opinion 41

Lesson 10: Using Cue Words: Literary Elements 44

Lesson 11: Using Text Evidence 47

Lesson 12: Justifying and Checking Your Answer 50

Lesson 13: Open-Ended Questions 53

Lesson 14: Using Test Time Effectively 56

Writing Test Strategies: Lessons and Practice

Lesson 15: Identifying Narrative Prompts 58

Lesson 16: Identifying Expository Prompts 60

Lesson 17: Identifying Persuasive Prompts 62

Lesson 18: Restating the Prompt 64

Lesson 19: Generating Your Thoughts 66

Lesson 20: Creating an Outline 68

Lesson 21: Understanding Evaluation Criteria 70

Reading Practice Tests

Level A, Test 1 74
Level A, Test 2 76
Level A, Test 3 78
Level A, Test 4 80
Level A, Test 5 82
Level A, Test 6 84
Level A, Test 7 86

Level B, Test 1 88
Level B, Test 2 92
Level B, Test 3 96
Level B, Test 4 98
Level B, Test 5 102
Level B, Test 6 108
Level B, Test 7 110

Writing Practice Tests

Narrative Writing Tests 116
Expository Writing Tests 119
Persuasive Writing Tests 122

Writing Prompts

Narrative Prompts 125
Expository Prompts 127
Persuasive Prompts 129

Additional Support

Rubrics 132
Answer Forms 136
Graphic Organizers 138
Resources 140
Classroom Management 143
Family Letters 145

Answer Key 147

Introduction to *Test-Taking Strategies*

Overview

Test-Taking Strategies equips struggling readers with useful strategies that will help them gain the confidence necessary to succeed on standardized tests. The materials build students' familiarity with the most widely used types of tests and question/answer formats.

The resources in this book are specifically designed to meet the needs of struggling readers in the *READ 180* classroom. Materials include the following:

- **Strategy Lessons** These lessons guide students in learning important test-taking strategies such as identifying literal and interpretive questions, using text evidence, and more. They provide direct instruction with modeling and guided practice to help students to master each strategy.

- **Passages and Practice Pages** Accompanying each lesson are practice activities that guide students to use strategies as they complete items covering a broad range of testing formats. Test items on many of the practice pages are based on passages of varied genres.

- **Leveled Reading Practice Tests** Practice tests are provided at two levels to scaffold students and promote early opportunities to experience success. Level A tests help familiarize students with test-taking situations, while promoting success through lower Lexile reading passages. Level B tests provide opportunities for students to practice with increasingly difficult texts.

- **Writing Practice Tests and Writing Prompts** Students practice the most widely assessed forms of writing, including:
  - Narrative
  - Expository
  - Persuasive

Throughout the lessons and practice materials, students are introduced to the most widely used formats and types of questions, including:
  - Multiple choice
  - Fill-in
  - Short answer
  - Open ended

Meeting Test-Taking Goals

Use resources in this book to meet your curriculum goals.

- Build students' test-readiness and confidence to help them succeed.

- Prepare for both curriculum and district-wide tests.

- Target instruction and practice to prepare for standardized tests and high-school exit exams.

- Meet state standards in reading and writing as you build familiarity with test formats and experiences.

- Address observed or assessed student needs.

See the following components for further instruction and practice to meet specific student needs in reading and writing:

1 RDI Book 1:
Reading Skills and Strategies

2 RDI Book 2:
Writing and Grammar Strategies

3 RDI Book 3:
Strategies for English-Language Learners

red Professional Development

Professional Development pages provide research-based information and practical, day-to-day tips for integrating test-taking materials into your instructional plans. Topics include:

- Building Student Confidence
- Reducing Text Anxiety
- Teaching Time-Management Skills
- Teaching Test-Taking Strategies
- Building Familiarity With Tests
- School-to-Home Communication

Additional Resources

Materials at the back of this book support instruction, assessment, and classroom management with resources such as the following:

- Assessment rubrics
- Graphic organizers
- Testing tips and brain booster activities
- Answer key
- Lesson tracking forms for classroom management
- Family letter

Prioritizing Instruction

Lessons may be used flexibly. You may wish to use them in sequence or to select specific strategies to meet specific student proficiency levels and instructional needs. In addition, lessons may be used to reinforce and extend test-taking strategies presented in each *rBook* Workshop.

rBook Workshop	Test-Taking Strategy	*Test-Taking Strategies* Page
Workshop 1, p. 30	Making an Educated Guess	page 18
Workshop 2, p. 54	Answering Fill-in-the-Blanks	page 21
Workshop 3, p. 80	Restating the Question	page 24
Workshop 4, p. 104	Previewing Questions	page 27
Workshop 5, p. 128	Literal and Interpretive Questions	page 33
Workshop 6, p. 160	Using Text Evidence	page 47
Workshop 7, p. 184	Using Cue Words	pages 38, 41, 44
Workshop 8, p. 208	Checking Your Answer	page 50
Workshop 9, p. 234	Justifying Your Answer	page 50

Using Curriculum-Based Assessment

The *rSkills Tests* that assess *rBook* comprehension, vocabulary/word study, and grammar skills may be used as low-stakes test practice opportunities. These tests are available in two levels to promote success. Guide students to practice test-taking strategies from this book as they take *rSkills Tests*.

(Continued on next page)

Overview of Resources

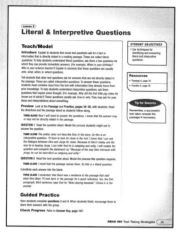

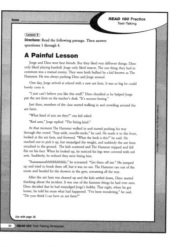

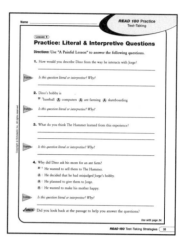

Lessons Present instruction for teaching students important test-taking strategies.

Passages Texts represent a variety of genres and content-area topics.

Strategy Practice Provides questions to guide students in practicing test-taking strategies.

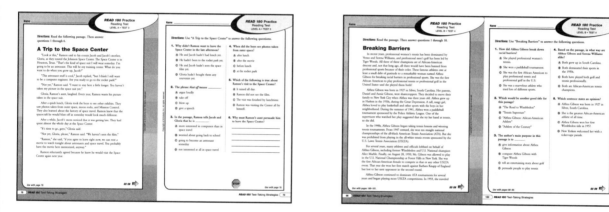

Leveled Reading Practice Tests Two levels of reading passages help scaffold students and provide the opportunity for success.

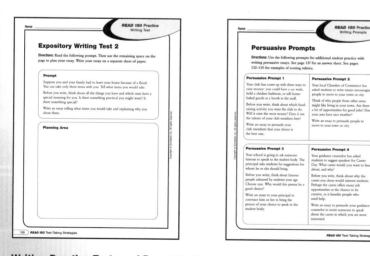

Writing Practice Tests and Prompts Provide student practice with the most widely assessed types of writing.

■SCHOLASTIC
red.

School-to-Home Communication

Students' families can provide valuable support for testing. Use these ideas to encourage family involvement.

- Use back-to-school nights, regular newsletters, conferences, and notices to keep families informed about testing throughout the year.

- Begin by giving families general information about test dates, names, and content.

- Explain how test results will be interpreted and share other forms of assessment such as the *READ 180* student reports.

- Give families practical ideas for helping students at home: talking about books, practicing time-management skills, setting up a place to study, and checking homework regularly.

- Send reminders and share testing tips, such as making sure students get enough sleep, have an adequate breakfast, and arrive on time for the test.

" *Scoring well on tests requires students to master content and skills as well as to show what they know on the test. Teach both to help students achieve higher test scores.* "

Dr. Richard K. Wagner

Assessment Tests and the Struggling Reader

"Adequate and appropriate test preparation plays an important role in helping students demonstrate their knowledge and skills in high-stakes testing situations" *(Gulek, 2003).*

Preparing for Tests

In order for students' test scores to reflect their concept and skill knowledge, preparation needs to include more than just test practice. Research shows that teaching test-taking strategies and test terminology improves student performance on high-stakes tests (Gulek, 2003; Marzano, Kendall, & Gaddy, 1999). The following five important types of high-stakes test preparation have been identified: teaching content-area concepts and skills, using varied assessment approaches and formats, teaching time-management skills, increasing student motivation, and reducing test-taking anxiety (Miyasaka, 2000).

Teaching Content-Area Curriculum

"In order to give students a fair chance to demonstrate what they know and can do, it is essential to expose them to all curriculum objectives to be mastered at their grade level" (Gulek, 2003). Regardless of test-taking skills, students will not earn acceptable test scores without adequate concept and skill knowledge in the content areas tested. The fundamental purpose of a high-stakes test is to provide evidence of concept and skill proficiency.

Instruction that addresses only those concepts and skills to be tested may raise scores, but such learning has limited benefits outside the context of the test. Moreover, the content of tests, such as college-entrance exams and civil-service exams, are not limited to the tested standards of a given state. Therefore, it is important to integrate test preparation with broader content-area learning. As students use *READ 180* to build phonemic awareness, phonics skills, fluency, vocabulary, comprehension, and writing skills, incorporate test-taking strategies into instruction to help them demonstrate their acquired knowledge and skills on high-stakes tests.

Instruction for Test Success

Good instruction is good test preparation. Much of the reading and writing instruction you provide may be integrated with test preparation, so that instructional time serves both purposes and you can avoid wasting time "teaching to the test." As you work with students to develop the reading and writing skills they need to succeed, you are also developing their ability to succeed on tests.

The following skills and strategies are developed throughout the components of *READ 180* and function to accelerate learning across the curriculum *and* to build test success:

- Development of rapid word recognition, leading to fluency, and an appropriate reading rate that facilitates comprehension.
- Reading, comprehending, and analyzing texts of varied text structures and genres.
- Building students' vocabulary, especially high-utility academic words that extend across content areas, such as those presented as Target Words in the *rBook*.
- Building students' ability to routinely use comprehension and self-monitoring strategies to help them make meaning from challenging text.
- Developing students' writing fluency in varied writing types, as well as their facility with using the most important writing conventions.

Teaching Test-Taking Strategies

"When struggling readers develop test-taking strategies, they build confidence for the test" (Taylor & Walton, 2001). In this book, students will learn strategies to help them attempt and complete most types of test questions.

Teach test-taking strategies that can be applied to tests in many content areas.

- Explain the importance of learning as much as possible about a test before taking it. For example, how much time is allowed? Are wrong answers, or a percentage thereof, subtracted from the score earned for correct answers? What types of questions are included? How many points are possible for each question or prompt?
- Explain and model the importance of reading and understanding all test directions.
- Practice reading directions from a sample state test and have your students restate them in their own words.
- Give examples of errors that could result from careless or incorrect reading of a question or direction.
- Model how to read and consider all multiple-choice answers before choosing one.
- Explain that students should answer every question on multiple-choice tests when there is no penalty for wrong answers.

- Let students know they should be sure they have marked their answers next to the correct number on their answer sheets. Caution them not to change answers without a good reason.

Resources

- Model how to read all questions and directions carefully. Teach students how to look for cue words, such as *compare* or *opinion,* and use them to understand what is being asked (pp. 38, 41, 44).
- Demonstrate how to preview questions before reading a passage to help students focus on relevant information as they read (p. 27).
- Teach and model how to look back in the passage for text evidence that supports the answer (p. 47).
- Model how to use the process of elimination to make an educated guess on multiple-choice items (p. 18). Even if wrong answers are penalized, eliminating one or more answer choices improves students' odds of guessing correctly.
- Stress the importance of justifying and checking answers to help students avoid careless errors (p. 50).

Integrating Test Preparation

"Ideally, integrated test preparation would mean that the strategies children most need to be successful on tests would be part of a teacher's daily instruction" (Taylor & Walton, 2001). Incorporating test-preparation strategies into *READ 180* will help students take tests in stride. Use of the practice tests in this book helps students make a smooth transition into an authentic test-taking situation.

- Integrate test preparation when a particular skill is taught so that students make the connection between what they learn and how it will be tested.
- Model and frequently remind students how to read and interpret directions for tasks throughout the day or class period.
- Review test results from the previous year to customize your teaching strategies.

Building Familiarity With Tests

"When students are familiar with the test format, terminology, and procedures, they are more likely to have positive test performances" (Taylor & Walton, 2001). Students may have mastered a concept, but if the test asks for it in a different format or using different vocabulary, they are sometimes unable to demonstrate their proficiency. Students need to be taught how to "read" a test in the same way that they need to be taught how to read different genres, such as poetry or nonfiction.

Follow these suggestions to help students become comfortable with the format of the test they will be given:

- Help students get to know the test format and types of questions asked. Use your state test format for quizzes or other questions that you assign as part of regular class work.
- Tell students how many points are possible for each question type or prompt. Explain how short responses, extended responses, and responses to writing prompts will be evaluated. If rubrics are available, show students how to earn partial credit even if they cannot answer every part of every question.
- Practice the test format regularly, using similar question types and prompts. For example, if the test requires short answers, have students practice writing short answers during regular writing activities.

- Analyze and explain models of both proficient and inadequate test answers with students.
- Explicitly teach students test vocabulary and terminology, such as words used in directions.
- Share general information about testing procedures, such as time limits and whether or not guessing is an effective strategy for a particular test.

Transition to Grade-Level Text

"Students become discouraged, frustrated, and intimidated and may not attempt the task when material is hard to read" (McCabe, 2000). Struggling readers are encouraged to read text at their level to build comprehension and fluency through extensive reading practice. When they take standardized tests, they are faced with a new challenge: applying their skills to grade-level text.

Use these strategies to help students make this transition:

- Build solid reading skills at students' instructional levels.
- Provide initial test-taking instruction and practice with materials at students' reading levels.
- Once students can apply test-taking strategies to material at their level, gradually help them apply their test-taking skills to grade-level passages.
- Remind students that they do not need to answer all questions correctly to achieve a passing score.
- Show students how they can earn credit by using strategies such as educated guesses for multiple-choice items and partial answers for written responses.

Changing Gears

"If unprepared for the disjointed, unconnected reading material of some tests, students with low test-taking self-efficacy may be unable to apply recently acquired test-taking skills and, as a result, may become frustrated and unable to respond correctly to questions they have the ability to answer" (McCabe, 2000). During classroom instruction, lessons usually focus on one genre or topic for an extended period of time to develop mastery. Teachers provide support before, during, and after reading. During a high-stakes test, it may be challenging for struggling readers to read a series of passages with different genres and topics in one sitting, especially with no instructional support.

Use these strategies to help students become accustomed to changing gears:

■ Explain that different genres and subjects call for different reading strategies.

■ After teaching a few text types or topics in depth, give students practice switching from one to another.

■ Include practice that requires students to extract information from charts or other graphic organizers.

Resources

■ As students work through different lessons, have them compare and contrast how they apply skills to different genres and subjects.

■ Provide practice changing gears between types of text (e.g., narrative/expository), topics, and content areas in a testing situation. Use a set of practice tests from this book in combination. For example, you might use "Soybeans" (p. 86), an expository selection with a chart; "Tallgirl Saves the Day" (p. 88), a short story with dialogue; and "Southbound on the Freeway" (p. 108), a poem.

Building Fluency

"If a state test requires students to write short responses to explain their reasoning, students would write frequently in this manner during the school year and receive feedback on their responses" (Taylor & Walton, 2001). In some high-stakes tests, written responses may account for a substantial percentage of the possible score. Short-answer questions, extended-response questions, and essays all require writing fluency. In addition, students must be able to write a coherent, organized response quickly in order to demonstrate proficiency on a timed test.

Use these strategies to build writing fluency within the context of a timed test:

■ Give students plenty of practice with writing in all subjects.

■ Introduce timed writing assignments, gradually increasing the amount of writing required within a given period.

■ Have students practice timed, unstructured writing. For example, have students write everything they can about a given topic in five minutes without concern for organization or conventions.

■ Introduce timed writing that is more structured and aims to meet the requirements. You can do this by setting time limits for varied tasks, such as responses to *rBook* React questions, QuickWrites, and other class work.

■ Emphasize the importance of writing in complete sentences. Encourage students to use complete sentences orally as they respond to questions in class, as well as in written responses to questions in their content-area textbooks.

Resources

■ Teach students how to respond to open-ended questions with short answers and extended responses (pp. 53, 58–69).

■ Use writing practice tests (pp. 116–124) to help students build writing fluency when responding to essay prompts. Begin with a generous time allowance and gradually reduce the allotted time.

■ Use writing prompts (pp. 125–130) to give students practice writing narrative, expository, and persuasive responses.

■ Have students monitor and learn to manage their use of test time. They may use Lesson 14, Tracker 2 (p. 57) to record time spent on the different tasks associated with completing writing test items.

■ Examine writing rubrics with students so that they know how written responses are likely to be evaluated (p. 70). Point out ways that they can earn partial credit if they are running short on time.

Preparing Students for On-Demand Writing

Many standardized tests require students to write on demand in response to a prompt. The amount of writing required may be anywhere from a few sentences to a complete essay. On-demand writing for extended responses are timed—students are given a defined amount of time to compose a polished piece in a specified writing type, such as expository/informative, narrative, or persuasive.

It is important to prepare students for tests that include on-demand writing, as the process and requirements of this type of writing differ from most classroom writing assignments. Please see the chart below for a comparison.

Helping Students Succeed

While on-demand writing has special requirements, you can integrate targeted test preparation into your regular writing instruction and practice. Some ways to do this include the following:

- Provide practice with timed writing by assigning time limits to regular work, such as QuickWrites and written responses to *rBook* React and Wrap-Up questions.
- Guide students to internalize the writing process with reminders that all writing involves *at least* three steps: (1) plan, (2) write, (3) revise and edit. Guide students to complete independent assignments, remembering to follow all three steps each time.

- Guide students to recognize their own use of time. Have them monitor how long each part of the writing process usually takes them. Which parts take the most time? What are ways they can work more efficiently?
- Provide regular practice in analyzing the writing prompt, so students learn to readily recognize the writing form and content that is expected.
- Assign writing practice tests and prompts from this book (pages 116–130). Assign time limits of gradually decreasing duration. Guide students to practice analyzing and responding to the prompts, gradually releasing the amount of support you provide.

Building Stamina and Focus

"Students with poor test-taking self-efficacy may be overwhelmed when presented with a test booklet containing many pages of material . . . An involuntary reaction of many students to this situation is an audible groan as lengthy test booklets are received or opened" (McCabe, 2000). Struggling readers may be used to reading at their own level, with frequent changes of pace. When taking a high-stakes test, they will face grade-level text and questions for an extended period of time.

These strategies will help build the stamina and focus needed for a lengthy high-stakes test:

- Have students read independently for increasingly long periods to build reading stamina.
- Build test-taking stamina by beginning with short selections and a few questions. Have students work for progressively longer periods using practice tests from this book and state test practice materials.

Supported Writing	On-Demand Writing
In-class writing often follows a writing process. Students are given several sessions to develop and polish their work until they have a final product that is to their satisfaction.	Students are able to plan and edit, but they must do so within a time limit and must manage the time on their own.
The writing process is usually scaffolded and guided by the teacher, and often involves peer feedback and support.	On-demand writing is an individual task. Students must develop their work without support or feedback from others.
The writing process is structured. The student is guided to follow specific steps, such as *brainstorm, prewrite/draft, revise,* and *publish.*	For on-demand writing, the student must remember to plan, write, edit, and revise without prompting, and must manage the amount of time it takes to complete each step.

- Have students practice about twice a week for four weeks as test time approaches. Gradually increase the duration of test practice. Begin with a testing period that is manageable for your students. You might begin with a fifteen-minute period of practice, gradually increasing by five- and then ten-minute intervals, until you build up to an hour.

- As you lengthen the practice period, add writing prompts until you achieve a balance of tasks that approximates the balance within your state test.

- Emphasize that a good night's sleep and a well-balanced breakfast will go a long way toward building focus and stamina.

- Explain that many people become tired during the test. Suggest that students deal with fatigue by stretching, breathing, rubbing their temples, and blinking their eyes. If permitted, drinking water or juice may be helpful.

- Tell students that when they are tired, the use of basic comprehension strategies can help them focus. They can use self-monitoring strategies to help them remember information and self-questioning strategies to check for understanding.

- Teach students to approach passages that don't engage their interest by identifying the genre and topic, previewing, and formulating questions to help search for information.

Teaching Time-Management Skills

"Students, including those with special needs, show improvement on tests when we teach time-management skills" (Jakupcak & Rushton, 1992). Once students have the stamina to persist through lengthy tests, they need to learn to manage their time effectively. Many factors can interfere with a student's ability to manage time in a testing situation. Some students worry about where others are on a test or rush through to demonstrate to peers that they are keeping up. Other students may not take the time to read test directions carefully.

Use these suggestions to address time-management issues:

- Administer timed practice tests throughout the year so that students become used to working within a time limit.

- Make sure students know that when they are stuck, they can mark the challenging question,

move on, and go back later. When doing so, they should be very careful to match the answer-sheet numbers with the test-item numbers.

- Teach students to preview the text and quickly establish a plan for how much time they should spend on multiple choice, short response, essays, and so on. You can model how to do this using a state practice test beforehand.

Resources

- Teach students to use test time effectively (p. 56).
- Have students use the Trackers in Lesson 14 to monitor their use of time during practice tests (p. 57).

Best Practices for Building Motivation and Confidence

"Student attitude and level of confidence toward testing significantly affect performance" (Roderick & Engel, 2001). Struggling readers are often uncomfortable about testing. Due to previous negative experiences with tests, some students may try to cope in ways that make the testing situation even more stressful. Even a student who displays confidence during regular class lessons may have difficulty when taking tests.

Lack of confidence can result in low scores even for students who read well and do well on classroom assignments (McCabe, 2000). Research also shows that motivation depends on a student's belief that personal effort leads to progress and mastery (Roderick & Engel, 2001). Therefore, it is especially important to teach students strategies to use in test situations and to provide positive reinforcement as students apply them.

Here are several ways that you can contribute to building students' confidence in their test-taking abilities:

- Provide frequent test-practice opportunities throughout the year to allow time for students to gain confidence, familiarity, and success with various tests.

- Integrate test practice with engaging content whenever possible, so that students are motivated to participate and succeed.

- Identify passages for practice based on students' interests.
- Set goals with students by determining their test-taking strengths and weaknesses. Set attainable, short-term goals and explain long-range objectives.
- Recognize and praise student successes often. To increase self-confidence, acknowledge improvements as they occur and provide immediate feedback.
- Attribute success to personal effort and specific behaviors so that students realize that they are responsible for progress. For example, saying "You earned a perfect score because you previewed the questions and looked for evidence in the passage" gives students confidence in their ability to affect results.
- Use charts and graphs to help students see individual progress. Visuals that compare early attempts with later attempts give students tangible evidence that they have improved.

Best Practices for Reducing Test Anxiety

"Preparing students for assessment tests reduces anxiety and builds their confidence, positively affecting their performance on assessment tests" (Gulek, 2003). Attaching high stakes to test results can increase test anxiety. Anxiety may interfere with comprehension during testing. Research shows that the higher a student's anxiety level, the lower the student's performance (Berliner & Casanova, 1988; Hancock, 2001; Smith, Arnkoff, & Wright, 1990). When students are anxious, they may become distracted and unable to concentrate.

This book provides leveled tests because many struggling readers become overwhelmed by the quantity of reading some tests require. The levels allow students to gain confidence by achieving success on lower-level tests before tackling grade-level tests.

When you are administering a high-stakes test, these strategies may reduce anxiety and help students feel more comfortable:

- Establish a calm, predictable routine for practice tests to set the tone for testing.
- Be aware of testing accommodations for English-language learners and students with special needs. Make arrangements ahead of time.
- Arrange desks carefully, keeping in mind students who might be distracted by or concerned with their peers.
- Whenever possible, administer the test in manageable sections, one at a time.
- Allow for one or more stretching breaks during testing.
- Model an optimistic attitude toward testing.
- Consider stress-reduction techniques for students, such as breathing, counting down from ten, and positive visualization.

Further Reading

Look up these professional articles for more information on preparing for assessment testing.

- Berliner, D., and Casanova, U. (1988). "How Do We Balance Test Anxiety and Achievement?" *Instructor,* 97(8), 14–15.
- Gulek, C. (2003). "Preparing for High-Stakes Testing." *Theory Into Practice,* 42(1), 42–50.
- Hancock, D. R. (2001). "Effects of Test Anxiety and Evaluative Threat on Students' Achievement and Motivation." *The Journal of Educational Research,* 94(5), 284–290.
- Jakupcak, J., and Rushton, R. (1992). *Corvallis School Inclusion Project (Report No. 141).* ERIC Document Reproduction Service No. ED357566.
- Marzano, R. J., Kendall, J. S., and Gaddy, B. B. (1999). *Essential Knowledge: The Debate Over What American Students Should Know.* Aurora, CO: McRel Institute.
- McCabe, P. (2000). "Enhancing Self Efficacy for High-Stakes Reading Tests." *Journal of Reading,* 51(1), 12–20.
- Miyasaka, J. R. (2000). "A Framework for Evaluating the Validity of Test Preparation Practices." Paper presented at the annual meeting of the American Educational Research Association, New Orleans.
- Roderick, M., and Engel, M. (2001). "The Grasshopper and the Ant: Motivational Responses of Low-Achieving Students to High-Stakes Testing." *Educational Evaluation and Policy Analysis,* 23(3), 197–227.
- Smith, R. J., Arnkoff, D., and Wright, T. (1990). "Test Anxiety and Academic Competence: A Comparison of Alternative Models." *Journal of Counseling Psychology,* 37(3), 313–321.
- Taylor, K., and Walton, S. (2001). "Testing Pitfalls (and How to Help Kids Avoid Them)." *Instructor,* 111(3), 23, 84–85.

How to Help Students Prepare for Exit Exams

Overview

All tests may be stressful for students, but exit exams may be even more so as they determine whether students will become high-school graduates or not. Failure may increase students' likelihood of dropping out. Sometimes this stress is enough to keep students from focusing and applying the skills they've developed. Using the materials in this book can help students prepare by building strategies and skills they need to face the test with increased confidence.

Following are some guidelines for addressing exit-exam anxiety.

Study the Test

Most states post exit exams from previous years on their Web sites. Share these with students to help them gain familiarity.

- **Test Language** Teach the specific test language that is used to frame questions and directions in your state tests. For example, the test might ask about a passage, "How was the issue resolved?" Students should realize that this simply means, "What was the solution to the problem?" Look at all types of questions and identify the specific cue words that your state test uses. Help students understand what each type of question is asking them to do.

- **Types of Questions** Review the types of questions and the different question formats on the test. Will the test be mostly multiple-choice? Will there be open-ended questions? Familiarity with test formats will make students less likely to feel overwhelmed when they face the test.

- **Expectations** Show samples of how students are to record their responses. Will they fill in bubbles? Write on lines? An understanding of what is expected will go a long way to helping students feel more confident in the actual test-taking situation.

- **Grading Criteria** Let students know what test graders will be looking for. Will they expect all essays to be five paragraphs? Will they use a specific rubric, or system to assign points and scores for writing complete sentences and paragraphs?

Focus on One Question a Day

Most teachers want to avoid having test preparation take the place of their regular curriculum. One way to accomplish this is to give students one practice test question a day right from the beginning of the school year. Each day, present a practice question, have the students respond, and then discuss in detail how they arrived at their answers. Ask questions such as:

- What is the test question asking you to do?
- How did you go about deciding on your answer?
- What else could you have done to help you get the correct answer?
- How can you check your answer?
- How can you use test time effectively?
- What's the most important thing you learned from today's practice question?

Pool answers and follow up with discussion and modeling. This will help build students' skills and prepare them to meet the challenges of the test.

Exit Exams Can Be Stressful

Students receiving reading and writing intervention are sometimes given materials that meet them at their skill level. The high school exit exam will not make many accommodations. Students will be asked to demonstrate grade-level skills; they will read more complex texts, and the passages will be longer. The test itself may be long, too. To help prevent students from "freezing up" as they encounter long tests and passages, use some of these strategies:

- **Build Reading Stamina** Provide practice with reading longer passages at the students' reading level, such as in Practice Test A in this book. As the test date nears, gradually increase the difficulty of the passages so that students have realistic ideas of what they will encounter (Practice Test B in this book).

- **Use Longer Passages** Let students know that they should identify and mark sections as they read—adding their own marginal notes. This will help "chunk" the passage into smaller sections and will help students find information when they return to the text to find answers to questions. (Before using this strategy, be sure that writing in the test booklet is permitted.)

- **Focus on One Part at a Time** Remind students to begin at the beginning and to take one step at a time. It is sometimes helpful to guide students to look over the length of the entire test in order to pace themselves.

If necessary, help students get information about tutoring and extra help provided by after-school or other programs in your community.

Incorporating these ideas into your instruction will help struggling readers develop better test-taking skills. With these tools, they will have the confidence to do their best in the face of this important, yet stressful, academic hurdle.

Strategy Lessons

Instruction and practice for useful test-taking strategies promote student success.

Reading Test Strategies: Lessons and Practice

Lesson 1: Making an Educated Guess 18
Lesson 2: Answering Fill-in-the-Blanks 21
Lesson 3: Restating the Question 24
Lesson 4: Previewing Questions 27
Lesson 5: Using Vocabulary Strategies 30
Lesson 6: Literal & Interpretive Questions 33
Lesson 7: Answering Proofreading Questions 36
Lesson 8: Using Cue Words: Compare, Cause/Effect 38
Lesson 9: Using Cue Words: Sequence, Fact/Opinion 41
Lesson 10: Using Cue Words: Literary Elements 44
Lesson 11: Using Text Evidence 47
Lesson 12: Justifying and Checking Your Answer 50
Lesson 13: Open-Ended Questions 53
Lesson 14: Using Test Time Effectively 56

Writing Test Strategies: Lessons and Practice

Lesson 15: Identifying Narrative Prompts 58
Lesson 16: Identifying Expository Prompts 60
Lesson 17: Identifying Persuasive Prompts 62
Lesson 18: Restating the Prompt 64
Lesson 19: Generating Your Thoughts 66
Lesson 20: Creating an Outline 68
Lesson 21: Understanding Evaluation Criteria 70

Lesson 1

Making an Educated Guess

STUDENT OBJECTIVES

- Use the process of elimination to make an educated guess.

Resources

- Passage 1, page 19
- Practice 1, page 20

Tip for Success

Remember, a successful test taker attempts to answer every question.

Teach/Model

Introduce Explain to students that a multiple-choice test has several different answer choices—usually four—for each question. Although several choices might seem possible, only one of those choices is correct. The student must identify that correct answer and indicate it by circling a letter or by filling in a bubble.

Suggest to students that they read all the answer choices, even if they think the first one is correct. As they read answer choices, they should cross out answers they know are wrong. Let them know that this is the process of elimination. Eliminating obviously wrong choices improves the odds of choosing the right one.

Tell students that if more than one choice remains, they should reread or skim the passage to look for words or phrases that give more support to one choice than another.

Preview Look at the **Passage** and **Practice, pages 19–20,** with students. Read the directions aloud.

> **THINK ALOUD** *I know that it is important for me to stay focused as I read so that I will understand what I am reading.*

Read the passage aloud while the students follow along.

> **THINK ALOUD** *I have read the passage. Now I can answer the questions.*

QUESTION 1 Read the question aloud. Model the process students might use to answer the question.

> **THINK ALOUD** *First I'll read the choices.* A *and* B *look like they could be right, but they do not summarize the entire passage. I can cross out choice* C *because this passage is really not about training dogs. So* D *seems to be the best choice.*

QUESTION 2 Read the sentence and answer choices aloud. Model the process this question requires.

> **THINK ALOUD** *Each of these choices could be a meaning for* pack. *Because this passage is about dogs, I can make an educated guess that the answer is* C, *but just in case, I'll check back in the text for how the word is used. Yes, in paragraph four, the second sentence provides the context clue to support the answer,* C.

Guided Practice

Have students complete **questions 3** through **5.** When students finish, encourage them to share their work with the group.

Check Progress Refer to **Answer Key, page 147.**

Lesson 1

Directions: Read the following passage. Then answer questions 1 through 5.

Dogs for Different Deeds

Which animal has been a pet throughout history? If you ask people around the world, they will probably answer, "dogs." Dogs are known for their intelligence, loyalty, and hard work. Different types of dogs are trained to perform different jobs.

Many people get dogs to guard their houses. Dogs do more than guard houses, though. Some work as seeing-eye dogs to guide people who are visually impaired. Some act as "ears" for people who are hearing impaired. Others <u>retrieve</u> items for people who are wheelchair-bound. Dogs may be helpful to hospital patients who need their spirits lifted. Some dogs help police officers find criminals. They do this by following the scent left from a piece of clothing. While people enjoy many other animals, dogs always have been a reliable source for work and emotional support.

Dogs make good pets because they are easy to train. Unlike cats or rabbits, they respond to commands and work for treats. Some dogs are trained to play roles in TV shows or movies. Dogs can learn to hunt, fetch, and pull. For example, huskies often haul sleds with supplies across the snowy fields of Alaska. Through hard work and patience, dogs can learn to do almost anything.

Because of the close relationship humans have with dogs, dogs treat humans as part of the dog's <u>pack</u>. The human family becomes the dog's family. Dogs are very loyal. When humans pet, feed, brush, walk, or play with their dogs, the dogs feel close to them. They are reminded of their instinct to stay close to their pack for protection in the wild. Since dogs are no longer wild, they look to people as their family group.

There are many reasons why dogs and humans have a close relationship. They enjoy working and playing together. Humans also value dogs for the safety they provide. It seems unlikely that dogs will ever be replaced as the favorite pet.

Use with page 20.

Lesson 1

Practice: Making an Educated Guess

Directions: Use "Dogs for Different Deeds" to answer the following questions.

1. Which is the best summary of this passage?

Ⓐ Dogs enjoy being cared for.

Ⓑ Dogs help people who are visually impaired or hearing impaired.

Ⓒ It is easy to train a dog.

Ⓓ Humans value dogs because of their helpfulness and loyalty.

2. In this article, what does the word *pack* mean?

Ⓐ to put things in a suitcase

Ⓑ a box of objects

Ⓒ a group or family

Ⓓ to fill completely

3. How do dogs help police officers?

Ⓐ They guard people's houses.

Ⓑ They protect people who cannot see.

Ⓒ They help them find criminals.

Ⓓ They follow them around.

4. In this article, what does the word *retrieve* mean?

Ⓐ to fetch

Ⓑ to haul

Ⓒ to obey

Ⓓ to roll over

5. What makes Alaskan huskies helpful dogs?

Ⓐ They help people who are hearing impaired.

Ⓑ They work as seeing-eye dogs.

Ⓒ They pull sleds through the snow.

Ⓓ They visit hospitals to cheer up people who are sick.

✓**CHECK** Did you read all of the choices before making your decision?

Use with page 19.

Lesson 2

Answering Fill-in-the-Blanks

Teach/Model

Introduce Explain that fill-in-the-blank questions require students to find the correct word or phrase to complete a sentence. Possible responses are listed in a multiple-choice format. Explain that when students complete a fill-in-the-blank, they need to read the sentence with each answer choice substituted into the blank to determine which one is correct. Remind students to use the strategy of making an educated guess. (See **pages 18–20**.)

Preview Look at the **Passage** and **Practice, pages 22–23,** with students. Read the directions aloud.

Read the passage aloud while the students follow along.

> **THINK ALOUD** *I've read the passage. Now I'll answer the questions. I understand that I need to choose the word or phrase that best completes each sentence.*

QUESTION 1 Read the question aloud. Then substitute each answer choice into the blank. Model the process students might use to answer the question.

> **THINK ALOUD** *I'll substitute each choice into the blank. Let me try the first one. "The Wright brothers learned about gliders by <u>watching the movements of birds</u>."*

Continue in the same manner with each choice.

> **THINK ALOUD** *There is nothing in the article about watching birds or reading about weather, so I can rule out choices A and D. The brothers had to learn about gliders before building one, so I can rule out C. So by using the process of elimination, that leaves B, and that answer is supported by a sentence in the first paragraph.*

QUESTION 2 Read the next question aloud substituting each answer. Model the process this question requires.

> **THINK ALOUD** *I know from the second paragraph that the first glider the Wright brothers built did soar in the sky, so C and D cannot be correct answers. I also learned that the glider had no engine. That means that B is not correct. So A is the right choice to complete the sentence.*

Guided Practice

Have students complete **questions 3** through **5.** When students finish, encourage them to share their work with the group.

Check Progress Refer to **Answer Key, page 147.**

STUDENT OBJECTIVES

- Substitute answer choices in the blank to determine which one is correct.

Resources

- Passage 2, page 22
- Practice 2, page 23

Tip for Success

Remember, a successful test taker eats a well-balanced breakfast on the morning of the test.

(Lesson 2)

Directions: Read the following passage. Then answer
questions 1 through 5.

The Wright Brothers

Wilbur and Orville Wright were brothers, born in Dayton, Ohio. They
dreamed of soaring across the open sky in a glider with an engine. They
never gave up on their dream. They read every book they could find on
gliders. Working in a shed behind their bicycle shop, they began to design
and build gliders of their own.

The first glider the Wright brothers built had no engine. Even so, it
soared on the wind like a plane. However, they realized the glider needed
a powerful engine to help keep it in the air longer. They also realized they
had to invent a way to make the glider rise up into the sky. They had to
find a way to turn it around while it was in the sky.

The brothers built a new glider. They decided to test it at Kitty Hawk,
North Carolina, where there were no buildings or trees to get in the glider's
way. The glider flew only a short distance, but Wilbur and Orville were
happy! They had learned how to control the glider's lift. Now the brothers
were ready to add steering. They designed and built another glider with
improved controls. They took turns practicing until they could steer it
perfectly.

Finally, they were ready to build the engine. It would have to be
lightweight but powerful. The brothers worked long and hard on the
engine. On December 17, 1903, again at Kitty Hawk, they tested their
engine-powered glider for the first time. It moved forward and then up into
the sky. Orville traveled 100 feet before he brought the glider down. When
Wilbur flew, he went twice as far as Orville. Wilbur then tried a second
time. He stayed in the air almost an entire minute, flying nearly 1,000 feet.
They had done it!

The Wright brothers turned their dream into a reality with a lot of hard
work, practice, and determination. Wilbur and Orville became pioneers of
flight. They laid the groundwork for modern air flight and the exploration
of space.

Use with page 23.

Lesson 2

Practice: Answering Fill-in-the-Blanks

Directions: Use "The Wright Brothers" to answer the following questions.

1. The Wright brothers learned about gliders by _____.

- Ⓐ watching the movements of birds
- Ⓒ building several gliders
- Ⓑ reading books about gliders
- Ⓓ reading books about weather

2. The first glider they built _____.

- Ⓐ had no engine
- Ⓒ fell to the ground
- Ⓑ had a small engine
- Ⓓ could not get off the ground

3. Orville and Wilbur chose Kitty Hawk as a place to test their gliders because _____.

- Ⓐ it was near their bicycle store
- Ⓒ it had no buildings or trees
- Ⓑ they had family and friends who lived there
- Ⓓ it was close to where they built and stored the gliders

4. The brothers needed an engine that would be _____.

- Ⓐ heavy and powerful
- Ⓒ lightweight but also powerful
- Ⓑ lightweight but not powerful
- Ⓓ built of steel

5. The trait that best describes the Wright brothers is _____.

- Ⓐ happy
- Ⓒ competitive
- Ⓑ calm
- Ⓓ determined

✓**CHECK** Did you substitute each answer choice in the blank before deciding which one was correct?

Use with page 22.

Lesson 3

Restating the Question

STUDENT OBJECTIVES

- Respond to short-answer questions by first restating the question as a statement, and then completing that statement with the correct answer.

Resources

- Passage 3, page 25
- Practice 3, page 26

Tip for Success

Remember, a successful test taker always reads the directions carefully.

Teach/Model

Introduce Tell students that to respond to a short-answer question, they should first restate the question as a statement that can be completed. For example, if a question asks, "Where do most whales live?" students should do the following:

- Restate the question as "Most whales live _____ ."

- Look in the passage for the information needed to complete the statement.

- Write the answer as a complete sentence: "Most whales live in the ocean."

Make sure students understand that the statement must directly answer the question.

Explain to students that for certain questions, called *interpretive questions*, the information needed to complete the statement will not be directly stated in the passage. Tell students that for this type of question, they will need to look in the passage for clues to help them complete their statement. (See **Lesson 6, pages 33–35,** for more about interpretive questions.)

Preview Look at the **Passage** and **Practice, pages 25–26,** with students. Read the directions aloud.

Read the passage aloud while the students follow along.

> **THINK ALOUD** *I have read the passage. Now I can answer the questions. These questions are not multiple-choice questions with answer choices. I must find information I need for each answer in the passage. I have to write the answers in complete sentences.*

QUESTION 1 Read the question aloud. Model the process students might use to answer the question.

> **THINK ALOUD** *First, I need to restate this question as a statement: "Jasmine wants to raise money because _____ ." Next, I need to find information in the passage to complete my statement. In the passage, the first sentence contains the information I need. I will use this information to write my answer: "Jasmine wants to raise money because she wants to buy a new stereo."*

Guided Practice

Have students complete **questions 2** through **6.** When students finish, encourage them to share their work with the group.

Check Progress Refer to **Answer Key, page 147.**

Lesson 3

Directions: Read the following passage. Then answer
questions 1 through 6.

Profit or Loss?

Jasmine had been eyeing a new stereo for months. She had a job at the
cafe, but it was closing. Jasmine was disappointed, but she knew things
would work out for her.

Jasmine was confident that she could find other ways to earn money.
Mostly, she was thinking of her grandmother's garage sale. But Jasmine
didn't want to sell any of her things, so she asked her grandmother if she
could fire up the grill and sell burgers to the customers.

"That's a great idea," her grandmother said. "It'll be like your own
private cafe around here."

On the day of the sale, Jasmine got the grill ready.

Just as the grill was ready, Jasmine's first customer arrived. "One
Double-Triple Burger," the man said, reading the sign. Jasmine got right
to work.

Soon the burgers really started moving. At first, she could barely keep
up. Then, she couldn't keep up at all. The customers became upset.

"I've been waiting half an hour," one complained.

"I'm starving," said another.

Suddenly Jasmine had an idea. She phoned her friend Carla. Jasmine
explained the situation. "If you help, I'll give you half of everything I
make." Jasmine said.

"Fine," Carla said.

Within no time, the duo chefs were cooking! After it was all over,
Jasmine and Carla had made serious money. Jasmine didn't quite have
enough for the stereo. But she was closer than before. And Carla was really
happy to have extra cash.

"Same time next year?" Jasmine asked.

"You got it," Carla replied.

Use with page 26.

Lesson 3

Practice: Restating the Question

Directions: Use "Profit or Loss?" to answer the following questions.

1. Why does Jasmine want to earn money?

_____

_____

2. Why does Jasmine's grandmother call the project "a private cafe?"

_____

_____

3. Why does Jasmine need Carla's help?

_____

_____

4. How does Jasmine convince Carla to help her?

_____

_____

5. What do Carla and Jasmine decide to do next year?

_____

_____

6. Based on Jasmine's actions, what kind of person do you think she is?

_____

_____

✓CHECK Did you begin each answer by restating the question as a statement?

Use with page 25.

Previewing Questions

Teach/Model

Introduce Explain to students that when taking a test, it is helpful to preview the questions before reading the passage. That way, as they read the passage, they will be able to zero in on the specific information they need to answer the questions. They will also be able to identify any paragraphs or other parts of the passage that do not directly relate to the questions.

Preview Look at the **Passage** and **Practice, pages 28–29,** with students. Read the directions aloud.

> **THINK ALOUD** *The directions tell me to read the poem and answer the questions. If I preview the questions first, I'll know just what to look for when I read the poem.*

Read the questions aloud while the students follow along.

> **THINK ALOUD** *Now as I read the poem, I will look for clues to help me answer the questions.*

Read the poem aloud while students follow along.

> **THINK ALOUD** *As I read, I found the clues I was looking for. Now I can answer the questions.*

QUESTION 1 Read the question aloud. Model the process students might use to answer the question.

> **THINK ALOUD** *Because I previewed this question, I was watching to see what made "the leaves hang trembling." The poem says that the leaves tremble when "the wind is passing thro'." So it is clearly the passing wind that is making them tremble. I'll restate the question as a statement and complete it with the information I found. My complete answer is: "In the poem, the wind makes the leaves tremble."*

Guided Practice

Have students complete **questions 2** and **3.** When students finish, encourage them to share their work with the group.

Check Progress Refer to **Answer Key, page 147.**

STUDENT OBJECTIVES

- Preview questions before reading the passage in order to know what to watch for while reading.

Resources

- Passage 4, page 28
- Practice 4, page 29

Tip for Success

Remember, if any test directions are not clear, a successful test taker asks questions.

(Lesson 4)

Directions: Read the following poem. Then answer questions 1 through 3.

Who Has Seen the Wind?
by Christina Rossetti

Who has seen the wind?
Neither I nor you:
But when the leaves hang trembling
The wind is passing thro'.

Who has seen the wind?
Neither you nor I:
But when the trees bow down their heads
The wind is passing by.

Use with page 29.

(Lesson 4)

Practice: Previewing Questions

Directions: Use "Who Has Seen the Wind?" to answer the following questions.

1. What makes "the leaves hang trembling" in the poem?

_____

_____

▶ Explain *Write the clues from the poem that support your answer.*

_____

_____

2. In this poem, the word *bow* means _____.

    Ⓐ a piece of ribbon   Ⓒ a weapon for shooting arrows

    Ⓑ to bend   Ⓓ a rainbow

▶ Explain *Write the clues from the poem that support your answer.*

_____

_____

3. What does the author mean in the second stanza when she uses the words, "their heads"?

_____

_____

▶ Explain *Write the clues from the poem that support your answer.*

_____

_____

✓ **CHECK** Did you preview the questions in order to know what to look for when you read?

Use with page 28.

Using Vocabulary Strategies

Resources

• Passage 5, page 31

• Practice 5, page 32

Tip for Success

Remember, a successful test taker has a positive attitude about the test.

Teach/Model

Introduce Explain to students that the way to answer vocabulary questions is to look for context clues that throw light on the meaning of the vocabulary word. Context clues may include the structure of the sentence that contains the word, examples or restatements that appear near the word, or facts and details that surround the word. (For example, *One important function of blood is to transfer, or carry, oxygen.*)

Sometimes the word itself offers a clue because it contains a word or a part that students may recognize: for example, *joyful, unwilling, topsoil.* Explain to students that this type of clue is called a *structural clue.* Encourage students to use both strategies when trying to figure out the definition of a word.

For vocabulary test questions, students should substitute the choices into the original sentence to see which makes sense. Then they can look back at the word in context and create a complete sentence that defines the word.

Preview Look at the **Passage** and **Practice, pages 31–32,** with students.

Read the directions and the passage aloud as students follow along.

QUESTION 1 Read the question aloud. Model the thinking process students might use to answer the question.

> **THINK ALOUD** Right *is an easy word, but it has many meanings. To find what meaning is meant here, I'll look for context clues.* Right *appears in this sentence: "At that time, Mexico still said it had an ownership* right *to Texas." I can tell that the word is being used as a noun, so I can eliminate choices* A *and* B *right away. Choice* D *makes no sense in the original sentence. For choice* C, *however, there is a context clue right in the next sentence: "Because of this claim . . ." So the answer must be choice* C, claim.

Read the sentence aloud while substituting the answer choice.

> **THINK ALOUD** Yes, when I substituted claim for right, it made sense.

Guided Practice

Have students complete **questions 2** and **3.** When students finish, encourage them to share with the group their thinking processes.

Check Progress Refer to **Answer Key, page 147.**

Lesson 5

Directions: Read the following passage. Then answer questions 1 through 3.

Texas Joins the United States

Texas was a separate nation for almost ten years before it became part of the United States in 1845. The United States hesitated before making Texas a state. The government <u>rejected</u> Texas's request to become a state in 1837 and again in 1844.

Why was the United States so uneasy about making Texas a state? At that time, Mexico still said it had an ownership <u>right</u> to Texas. Because of this claim, American officials worried that bringing Texas into the United States might lead to war with Mexico. Also, Texas had debts from its war with Mexico. If Texas were a state, the United States would have to help pay those debts. So, the United States said no.

Some Texans wanted to keep their independence. Texas's second president, Mirabeau Lamar, tried to convince Texans that they would be better off as a separate nation. However, most Texans had moved to Texas from other states. They believed that joining a large nation would help them to grow and <u>prosper</u>.

Sam Houston was president of the Republic of Texas before and after Lamar. He worked hard to get Texas into the United States. When Anson Jones became president of Texas in 1844, a new request was sent to Washington. According to this request, Texas would pay its own debts. There were still <u>disputes</u> with Mexico about Texas's borders. But the United States agreed to settle these arguments.

The United States approved the new request on December 29, 1845. Back then, news took time to travel. Texas continued as a republic until a ceremony on February 19, 1846. On that day, Anson Jones stepped down as president of Texas. He welcomed the state's first governor. The U.S. flag was raised over Texas. At long last, Texas became part of the United States of America.

Use with page 32.

Lesson 5

Practice: Using Vocabulary Strategies

Directions: Use "Texas Joins the United States" to answer the following questions.

1. In the second paragraph, the word <u>right</u> means _____.

    Ⓐ true   Ⓒ claim

    Ⓑ good   Ⓓ the opposite of left

▶**Explain** *Write the clues from the passage that helped you to understand the meaning of <u>right</u>.*

_____

_____

2. In the first paragraph, what does the word <u>rejected</u> mean?

_____

_____

▶**Explain** *Write the clues from the passage that helped you to understand the meaning of <u>rejected</u>.*

_____

_____

3. In the fourth paragraph, the word <u>disputes</u> means _____.

    Ⓐ defeats   Ⓒ allowances

    Ⓑ arguments   Ⓓ reputations

▶**Explain** *Write the clues from the passage that helped you to understand the meaning of <u>disputes</u>.*

_____

_____

✓**CHECK** Did you check your answer by substituting in the passage?

Use with page 31.

Lesson 6

Literal & Interpretive Questions

Teach/Model

Introduce Explain to students that some test questions ask for a fact or information that is directly stated in a reading passage. These are called *literal questions.* To help students understand literal questions, ask them a few questions for which they can provide immediate answers. (For example, *When is your birthday? Who is your science teacher?*) Explain to students that these questions are usually *who, what, when,* or *where* questions.

Tell students that other test questions ask for answers that are not directly stated in the passage. These are called *interpretive questions.* To answer these questions, students must combine clues from the text with information they already know from prior knowledge. To help students understand interpretive questions, ask them questions that require some thought. (For example, *Why did the first little pig make his house out of sticks?*) These questions usually ask *how* or *why.* They may ask for your ideas and interpretations about something.

Preview Look at the **Passage** and **Practice, pages 34–35,** with students. Read the directions and the passage aloud as students follow along.

> **THINK ALOUD** *Now I will need to answer the questions. I know that the answer may or may not be directly stated in the passage.*

QUESTION 1 Read the question aloud. Model the process students might use to answer the question.

> **THINK ALOUD** *The author does not describe Dino in the story. So this is an interpretive question. I'll have to look for clues in the text. I know that I can use the dialogue between Dino and Jorge for clues. Because of Dino's hobby and the way he is teasing Jorge, I can infer that he is outgoing and witty. I will restate the question and complete the statement as: "Because of the way Dino interacts with Jorge, he can be described as outgoing and witty."*

QUESTION 2 Read the next question aloud. Model the process this question requires.

> **THINK ALOUD** *I recall that the passage names them. So this is a literal question.*

Substitute each answer into the blank.

> **THINK ALOUD** *I remember that there was a sentence in the passage that said what Dino liked. I'll look back in the passage for a quick reference. Yes, the first paragraph, third sentence, says that he "liked playing baseball." Choice A is the answer.*

Guided Practice

Have students complete **questions 3** and **4.** When students finish, encourage them to share their answers with the group.

Check Progress Refer to **Answer Key, page 147.**

STUDENT OBJECTIVES

- Use techniques for identifying and answering literal and interpretive questions.

Resources

- Passage 6, page 34
- Practice 6, page 35

Tip for Success

Remember, a successful test taker rereads the passage if necessary.

Name _____

Lesson 6

Directions: Read the following passage. Then answer
questions 1 through 4.

A Painful Lesson

Jorge and Dino were best friends. But they liked very different things. Dino
only liked playing baseball. Jorge only liked insects. The one thing they had in
common was a mutual enemy. They were both bullied by a kid known as The
Hammer. He was always pushing Dino and Jorge around.

One day, Jorge arrived at school with a new ant farm. It was so big he could
barely carry it.

"I just can't believe you like this stuff," Dino chuckled as he helped Jorge
put the ant farm on the teacher's desk. "It's sooooo boring."

Just then, members of the class started walking in and crowding around the
ant farm.

"What kind of ants are they?" one kid asked.

"Red ants," Jorge replied. "The biting kind."

At that moment The Hammer walked in and started pushing his way
through the crowd. "Step aside, noodle-necks," he said. He made it to the front,
looked at the ant farm, and frowned. "What the heck is this?" he said. He
reached out to pick it up, but misjudged the weight, and suddenly the ant farm
smashed to the ground. The kids scattered and The Hammer tripped and fell
flat on his face. When he looked up, he noticed his legs were covered with red
ants. Suddenly, he realized they were biting him.

"Aaaaaaaaaahhhhhhhhhhhh," he screamed. "Get them off me." He jumped
up and tried to brush them off, but it was no use. The Hammer ran out of the
room and headed for the showers in the gym, screaming all the way.

After the ant farm was cleaned up and the kids settled down, Dino started
thinking about the incident. It was one of the funniest things he had ever seen.
Dino decided that he had misjudged Jorge's hobby. That night, when he got
home, he told his mom what had happened. "I've been wondering," he said.
"Do you think I can have an ant farm?"

Use with page 35.

Lesson 6

Practice: Literal & Interpretive Questions

Directions: Use "A Painful Lesson" to answer the following questions.

1. How would you describe Dino from the way he interacts with Jorge?

_____

Explain ▶ *Is this question literal or interpretive? Why?*

_____

2. Dino's hobby is _____.

Ⓐ baseball   Ⓑ computers   Ⓒ ant farming   Ⓓ skateboarding

Explain ▶ *Is this question literal or interpretive? Why?*

_____

3. What do you think The Hammer learned from this experience?

_____

_____

Explain ▶ *Is this question literal or interpretive? Why?*

_____

4. Why did Dino ask his mom for an ant farm?

Ⓐ He wanted to sell them to The Hammer.

Ⓑ He decided that he had misjudged Jorge's hobby.

Ⓒ He planned to give them to Jorge.

Ⓓ He wanted to make his mother happy.

Explain ▶ *Is this question literal or interpretive? Why?*

_____

✓CHECK Did you look back at the passage to help you answer the questions?

Use with page 34.

Answering Proofreading Questions

STUDENT OBJECTIVES

- Proofread and correct mistakes in spelling, grammar, and mechanics.

Resources

- Practice 7, page 37

Tip for Success

Remember, a successful test taker concentrates on his or her own work and doesn't worry about how others are doing.

Teach/Model

Introduce Explain to students that proofreading involves finding and correcting mistakes in writing. Point out to students that whenever they read a passage on a test, they should pay close attention to the spelling, grammar, and mechanics that the writer uses. Even if the passage seems to make sense, it pays to go back and check these elements.

Recommend to students that they sharpen their proofreading skills by practicing finding and correcting mistakes in their own or others' writing.

Preview Look at the **Practice, page 37,** with students. Read the directions aloud.

> **THINK ALOUD** *The directions tell me I must read the passage and decide which type of error, if any, appears in each underlined section. The errors may be in spelling, punctuation, capitalization, or grammar. I must select the answer that corrects each error.*

Read the passage aloud while the students follow along.

> **THINK ALOUD** *As I read the passage, I will pay close attention to the underlined sections. What error does each one show? How would I correct it?*

QUESTION 1 Read the first underlined passage section aloud. Then read the four possible ways of correcting it shown. Model the process students might use to answer this question.

> **THINK ALOUD** *Looking at the underlined section, I see that* is *is a singular verb but the subject,* bobsleds, *is plural. This means that the subject and verb do not agree. The plural of* is *is* are. *Choice C changes* is *to* are *without introducing any other error. On the line below, I'll write* grammar *to tell the kind of error that appeared.*

Guided Practice

Have students complete **questions 2** through **4.** When they are finished, encourage them to share their work with the group.

Check Progress Refer to **Answer Key, page 147.**

Name _____

Lesson 7

Practice: Proofreading Questions

Directions: Read the passage. Decide whether each underlined area contains an error. If so, mark the answer that corrects it. If not, mark "No Mistake."

Bobsledding is a very popular winter sport. Bobsleds, which are made

of <u>steel, is designed</u> to glide down ice-covered slopes at high speed.
    (1)

A famous bobsled run is located in <u>Lake placid, New York</u>. The sleds can be
                                    (2)

from nine to twelve feet and can seat four people. They range in <u>wait</u> up to
                                                                   (3)

500 pounds. Fans <u>say "Bobsledding</u> is the most exciting winter sport."
                 (4)

1. Ⓐ Steel, are designed
Ⓑ steel is designed
Ⓒ steel, are designed
Ⓓ No Mistake

2. Ⓐ Lake Placid, New York
Ⓑ lake placid, New York
Ⓒ lake Placid, New York
Ⓓ No Mistake

Explain *What type of error appeared?*

Explain *What type of error appeared?*

_____

_____

3. Ⓐ wate
Ⓑ weight
Ⓒ waite
Ⓓ No Mistake

4. Ⓐ say, "Bobsledding
Ⓑ say. "Bobsledding
Ⓒ say Bobsledding
Ⓓ No Mistake

Explain *What type of error appeared?*

Explain *What type of error appeared?*

_____

_____

✓CHECK Did you choose the answer that fixes the mistake?

Use with page 36.

Lesson 8

Using Cue Words: Compare, Cause/Effect

STUDENT OBJECTIVES

- Use cue words to determine if a compare/contrast answer is expected.
- Use cue words to determine if a cause/effect answer is expected.

Resources

- Passage 8, page 39
- Practice 8, page 40

Tip for Success

Compare/ Contrast Cue Words	Cause/ Effect Cue Words
same	because
similar	since
like	result
both	reason
as	so
also	if...then
too	due to
unlike	leads to
but	therefore
more	
less	
better	
worse	
different	
although	
however	
on the other hand	

Teach/Model

Introduce Tell students that to answer a test question, they must first determine the type of answer that is expected. Point out that one strategy is to look for cue words in the question such as *compare, contrast* or *cause, effect*. Explain that recognizing common text structures, or how the text is organized, can also help students find information and avoid rereading text that does not relate to the question.

Review that *compare* means "to tell how things are alike." *Contrast* means "to tell how things are different." So if students see *compare* or *contrast* in a question, they should know that they are expected to choose or write an answer that tells how things are alike or different. List other words or phrases that may signal comparison or contrast.

Explain that other questions may require students to find causes and effects. If students see the words *why, cause,* or *effect* in a question, the answer should tell what makes something happen or what results from something else. Students should then scan the passage for cause-and-effect relationships and cue words that identify them. List other words or phrases that may signal cause or effect.

You may wish to post a chart of cue words for future reference. Explain that other words can function as cue words, and that sometimes cue words are not used at all.

Preview Look at the **Passage** and **Practice, pages 39–40,** with students. Read the directions aloud.

> **THINK ALOUD** *Before I read, I will preview the questions and look for cue words to help me figure out exactly what the questions ask.*

Read the passage aloud. Encourage students to raise their hands when they recognize cue words that tell them what type of information is in the sentence or paragraph.

Question 1 Read the question aloud. Model how to think about the question.

> **THINK ALOUD** *I previewed this question and saw the cue word* why, *so I know I should look for the cause or reason why the moon appears to change shape. I see the word* reason *in the sentence, "This reflected light is the reason the moon appears in different shapes and sizes." This does not completely explain the cause, so I read further. I see the word* because *in this sentence: "It only seems to change because we see the bright side of the moon from different directions over the course of a month." Now I can restate the question and use these supporting details. My answer will be: "The reason the moon appears in different shapes and sizes is that we see the bright side of the moon from different directions over the course of a month. The passage says that when the moon shines, it is reflecting light from the sun and that it does not really change shape."*

Guided Practice

Have students complete **questions 2** and **3.** Then have them share their work.

Check Progress Refer to **Answer Key, page 147.**

Name _____

Lesson 8

Directions: Read the following passage. Then answer questions 1 through 3.

The Sun

The sun is one of billions of stars in the universe. Like all other stars, it is made up of hot gases that produce light and heat. To people on Earth, the sun is more important than any other star. If the sun did not provide heat and light, then life could not exist on Earth. Because of how the sun rotates, scientists can tell it is not a solid body but is made of gases. The sun's rotation period at its equator is about 25 days. At its poles the period is about 31 days. By contrast, the rotation period of a solid body such as Earth is the same at every point on its surface. Only a very small fraction of the sun's light and heat, one part out of two billion, reaches the Earth. The rest is lost in space. Yet what reaches us is enough to light up the entire sky during the day.

The Moon

The moon is Earth's closest neighbor in space, so it was the first object in space to be visited by human beings. The moon's diameter is 400 times smaller than the sun's, and the moon weighs 80 times less than the Earth. It takes the moon about 29 1/2 days to revolve around the Earth. Unlike the Earth, the moon does not rotate on its axis. The same side of the moon always faces Earth, and the other side always faces away from Earth. The moon is made of ground-up rocks, bits of glass, and scattered chunks of rock. It is dark gray to brown in color. The brightly shining moon is a beautiful sight in the night sky. Yet when the moon shines, it is actually reflecting light from the sun. This reflected light is the reason the moon appears in different shapes and sizes. It does not really change shape. It only seems to change because we see the bright side of the moon from different directions over the course of a month.

Use with page 40.

Lesson 8

Practice: Using Cue Words

Directions: Use "The Sun" and "The Moon" to answer the following questions.

1. Why does the moon appear to change in shape?

_____

_____

_____

Explain ▶ *Write the cue word that helps you know what kind of answer is expected.*

_____

2. How does the passage compare the sun to all other stars?

   Ⓐ It says that the sun rotates

   Ⓒ It says they are all the same size. in about 25 days.

   Ⓑ It says that the sun is one of billions of stars.

   Ⓓ It says they are all made up of hot gases.

Explain ▶ *Write the cue word that helps you know what kind of answer is expected.*

_____

3. What is the difference between the sun's rotation and the rotation of the earth?

_____

_____

Explain ▶ *Write the cue word that helps you know what kind of answer is expected.*

_____

✓CHECK Did you use cue words to help you find the correct answer?

Use with page 39.

Lesson 9

Using Cue Words: Sequence, Fact/Opinion

Teach/Model

Introduce Remind students that to answer a test question, they must first determine the type of answer that is expected. A good strategy is to look in the question for cue words such as *sequence, order, first, fact,* and *opinion.* Explain that recognizing common text structures can also help students find information and avoid rereading text that does not relate to the question.

> **THINK ALOUD** *The word* sequence *means "the order in which events take place." So if I see words such as* sequence, order, *or* first *in a question, I will choose or write an answer that tells the order in which steps or events take place.*

List words or phrases that may signal time order in a question or passage.

Explain that the words *fact* or *opinion* in a question suggest that the answer should distinguish fact from opinion. Review that a *fact* is a true statement. It can be proved or checked. An *opinion* is a statement of what someone believes or feels. Although it may make sense, seem fair, or seem morally right, it cannot be checked or proved. List cue words and phrases that signal fact and opinion.

You may wish to post a chart of cue words for future reference. Explain that other words can function as cue words, and that sometimes cue words are not used at all.

Preview Look at the **Passage** and **Practice, pages 42–43,** with students. Read the directions aloud.

> **THINK ALOUD** *Before I read, I will preview the questions so that I can use the cue words to help me find the correct information.*

Read the passage aloud. Encourage students to raise their hands when they recognize cue words that tell them what type of information is in the sentence or paragraph.

Question 1 Read the question aloud. Model how to think about the question.

> **THINK ALOUD** *Because I previewed this question and saw the cue word* opinion, *I knew I should look for a statement of what somebody thinks or feels. In that case, it cannot be choice* A, B *or* D. *They can be checked. I could not check or prove choice* C. *It must be an opinion, so I will mark it as my answer.*

Question 2 Read the next question aloud. Follow the process used for question 1.

> **THINK ALOUD** *This text is in time order, so I'll look at the beginning for the answer. The word* before *tells me to look for the order in which events took place. I found the word* had *in the second sentence of paragraph 2, which tells me this happened before the other events in the paragraph. My answer will be: "His father had played the violin in a band on the plantation where he had been a slave."*

Guided Practice

Have students complete **questions 2** and **3.** Have them share their work.

Check Progress Refer to **Answer Key, page 147.**

STUDENT OBJECTIVES

- Use cue words to determine if a fact/opinion answer is expected.
- Use cue words to determine if a sequence answer is expected.

Resources

- Passage 9, page 42
- Practice 9, page 43

Tip for Success

Use these cue words to help identify the kind of answer that is expected.

Sequence Cue Words	Opinion Cue Words
first	think
next	feel
last	believe
finally	should
then	must
during	seem
now	good
as	better
while	best
already	wonderful
recent	nice
earlier	beautiful
later	bad
until	worse
by	worst
since	terrible
following	more
soon	most
at the same time	less
	least
	greatest

(Lesson 9)

Directions: Read the following passage. Then answer
questions 1 through 3.

Scott Joplin
by Marcelle Stern

Scott Joplin was an extraordinary figure in the history of American music. He
was one of the originators of ragtime, a style of music that was a forerunner of jazz.
He was also, arguably, its greatest composer.

Joplin was born in 1868. His father had played the violin in a band on the
plantation where he had been a slave. Joplin's mother was a wonderful singer. She
accompanied herself on the banjo. During young Scott's childhood he was
constantly surrounded by music, and he decided to take up the piano.

While still in his teens, Scott left home to become a professional musician. In
1885 he ended up in St. Louis, Missouri. In St. Louis, he met musicians who were
playing pieces called rags. They were derived mainly from popular songs, but played
in an offbeat rhythm called ragtime. That rhythm put stresses in what sounded like
all the wrong places. It made the tunes exciting to dance to.

Fascinated by ragtime, Joplin decided to become a composer. He began to
perform regularly at the Maple Leaf Club. Later, in 1899, Joplin published his first
important work, called "Original Rags." A publisher named John Stark published
more of Joplin's works. Within a few years, Joplin became famous.

Joplin hoped that his pieces would be considered art, and that his music might
be played in concert halls someday. He wrote some long dance pieces that were like
mini-ballets. He even wrote a full-scale opera, *Treemonisha*, but he couldn't find any
large producer for it. The rest of Joplin's life is a sad story. His music was popular for
a while, but it was not performed in concert halls during his lifetime.

But then, in the 1970s, a new generation of musicians discovered Scott Joplin's
music. Before long, his rags were being played in concerts and used in movies. His
longer pieces have inspired many ballets. *Treemonisha* eventually succeeded on the
opera-house stage. Today, the sounds of ragtime can be heard everywhere.

Use with page 43.

Name _____

Lesson 9

Practice: Using Cue Words

Directions: Use "Scott Joplin" to answer the following questions.

1. Which statement in the second paragraph is an opinion?

   Ⓐ Joplin was born in 1868.

   Ⓑ His father had played the violin in a band on the plantation where he had been a slave.

   Ⓒ Joplin's mother was a wonderful singer.

   Ⓓ She accompanied herself on the banjo.

Explain ▶ *Write the cue word that helps you know what kind of answer is expected.*

_____

2. Which event in this biography happened before Joplin was born?

_____

_____

Explain ▶ *Write two cue words that help you know what kind of answer is expected.*

_____

3. Find an opinion in the next-to-last paragraph. List a fact that the writer states to support the opinion.

_____

_____

_____

Explain ▶ *Write the cue words that help you know what kind of answer is expected.*

_____

✓CHECK Did you use cue words to help you think about the question?

Use with page 42.

Lesson 10

Using Cue Words: Literary Elements

STUDENT OBJECTIVES

- Identify cue words that signal answers relating to literary elements.

Resources

- Passage 10, page 45
- Practice 10, page 46

Tip for Success

Remember, a successful test taker keeps track of the time.

Teach/Model

Introduce Remind students that to answer a test question correctly, they must first determine the type of answer that is expected. A good strategy is to look in the question for cue words.

Explain that when students find fiction passages and questions, they should look for cue words about literary elements such as plot and character. List cue words relating to character:

Traits	Motives	Words	Conflict	Moral, or Theme
describe	why	say	problem	moral
trait	want	said	conflict	point
characteristics	reason	think	solution	meaning
quality	purpose	respond	solve	lesson
personality	try	dialogue	resolve	message

You may wish to post a chart of cue words for future reference. Explain that other words can function as cue words, and that sometimes cue words are not used at all.

Preview Look at the **Passage** and **Practice, pages 45–46,** with students. Read the directions aloud. Then notice that the passage is a Greek myth. Explain that this signals that it is fiction and that they should read for information about the character and plot.

Question 1 Read the question aloud. Model how to think about the question.

THINK ALOUD *Because this question includes the cue word* lessons, *I knew I should think about what worked and did not work for the characters in the story and how it ended. Answer choice* A *is a good lesson but I must check the other choices first.* B *and* C *are not about what happened in the story. Melanion did use teamwork, but* A *is a better lesson for this story than* D. *I will mark* A *as my answer.*

Question 2 Read the next question aloud. Follow the process used for question 1.

THINK ALOUD *The word* say *tells me to look for Atalanta's words, so I should look for quotation marks or a word such as* said. *The phrase* after the race *tells me to look for the answer in the end of the story. My answer will be:* "Atalanta said, 'You are not faster than I am, but you found a way to slow me down. I will marry you.'"

Guided Practice

Have students complete **questions 2** and **3.** Encourage them to share their work with the group.

Check Progress Refer to **Answer Key, page 147.**

Lesson 10

Directions: Read the following passage. Then answer
questions 1 through 3.

Atalanta and the Golden Apples
A Greek Myth

Atalanta distrusted men. When she was a baby, her father, who wanted a boy, abandoned her on a mountaintop. A bear found the crying child and raised her with her own cubs. Years later, some hunters found Atalanta in the forest and raised her themselves. Atalanta became an outstanding hunter and an amazing runner. By the age of 9, she could outrun any hunter. By 15, she could run as fast as a deer.

Atalanta believed she would never love a man. One day at the Temple of Artemis, the goddess of the hunt, Atalanta made a vow: "I will never marry." As soon as men heard that Atalanta would never marry, they wished to marry her. Atalanta wanted to scare off suitors, but now she had dozens. Needing a new strategy, she revised her vow. She said, "I will marry only a man who can outrun me in a race." She knew she could never lose. "I will even give any challenger a lead."

Men came from far and near to race Atalanta. At every race Atalanta allowed the suitor to begin almost halfway to the finish line. Atalanta won every race. Melanion watched Atalanta vanquish one suitor after another. He was in love, and he begged the goddess Aphrodite for help. Believing that Atalanta was wrong to reject love and marriage, Aphrodite agreed to help by giving him three golden apples.

Melanion started the race far ahead of Atalanta. A bag tied at his waist held the three golden apples. At the signal, both runners hurtled forward. Melanion heard Atalanta's swift steps close behind him. He grabbed a golden apple and tossed it behind him. Atalanta stopped to pick it up while Melanion charged ahead. Holding the precious apple, Atalanta continued running.

Soon, Melanion heard Atalanta's feet behind him, and he tossed the second golden apple. Again, Atalanta stopped to pick it up. With an apple in each hand, Atalanta had to slow down, but still she nearly caught up to Melanion.

Melanion tossed his third apple to the side. It rolled off the racecourse, but the golden fruit was so beautiful that Atalanta ran after it. Melanion was close to winning. With all her power, Atalanta grasped the three apples and dashed to the finish line.

Melanion crossed the line an instant before Atalanta. He had won! Atalanta said, "You are not faster than I am, but you found a way to slow me down. I will marry you." Melanion beamed as he whispered his thanks to the goddess Aphrodite.

Use with page 46.

(Lesson 10)

Practice: Using Cue Words

Directions: Use "Atalanta and the Golden Apples" to answer the following questions.

1. Which of these lessons is supported by this story?

   Ⓐ A clever strategy can make the impossible possible.

   Ⓑ Love gives wings to the feet of the lover.

   Ⓒ Running away from your problems never solves anything.

   Ⓓ It takes teamwork and persistence to get any job done.

▷ Explain *Write the cue word that helps you know what kind of answer is expected.*

_____

2. After the race, what did Atalanta say about how Melanion won?

_____

_____

▷ Explain *Write two cue words that help you look for the answer.*

_____

3. What problem did Melanion need to solve?

_____

_____

▷ Explain *Write the cue word that helps you know what kind of answer is expected.*

_____

✓ CHECK Did you use cue words to help you find the correct answer?

Use with page 45.

Using Text Evidence

Teach/Model

Introduce Explain to students that the correct answer to a reading test question will always be supported by evidence in the text, or passage. As a result, they should always be certain that any answer they choose or write has evidence in the passage to support it.

Help students recall that *interpretive questions,* which ask about something not directly stated in the text, require them to return to the passage to look for evidence to connect with their prior knowledge to answer the question. Remind them that this process is called *making an inference.*

Preview Look at the **Passage** and **Practice, pages 48–49,** with students. Read the directions aloud.

> **THINK ALOUD** *Before I read the passage, I am going to preview the questions. It will help me read for the correct information.*

Read the passage aloud while students follow along.

> **THINK ALOUD** *I have read the passage. Now I can start answering the questions. I will make sure that there is evidence in the passage for every answer I choose or write.*

QUESTION 1 Read the question aloud. Model the process students might use to answer the question.

> **THINK ALOUD** *The passage states that Keesha screamed when she saw the "leaping lunch bag." Her reaction is also punctuated with exclamation marks. Looking at both of these clues, I can infer that she was surprised and/or shocked. I will restate the question and complete the statement as: "Shawna's sister, Keesha, was surprised when she saw the leaping lunch bag."*

Guided Practice

Have students complete **questions 2** and **3.** When students finish, encourage them to share their work with the group.

Check Progress Refer to **Answer Key, page 147.**

STUDENT OBJECTIVES
- Use text evidence to support answers to questions about a passage.

Resources
- Passage 11, page 48
- Practice 11, page 49

Tip for Success

Remember, a successful test taker is very careful to make the question and answer numbers line up when filling in an answer on a bubble answer sheet.

(Lesson 11)

Directions: Read the following passage. Then answer
questions 1 through 3.

The Leaping Lunch Bag

Shawna and her family had taken a picnic lunch to Daytona Beach.
The family had just moved to Florida from New York, and they were eager
to see the nice Florida beaches. The sun was shining, and it was a beautiful,
warm April day. However, the ocean was far from warm.

"Yikes! It's freezing," Shawna screamed as she raced out of the water.

Shawna walked up to the spot where the family had left their towels
and picnic blanket. She wrapped a towel around herself and thought,
"That's better!" Then she looked at the pile of brown paper bags on the
picnic blanket. Immediately Shawna knew that something was wrong.

"Mom!" Shawna called. "Didn't you pack enough lunches?"

"Of course I did, Shawna," Mom replied. "We counted them before we
loaded the car, remember?"

"Yes, I remember," Shawna answered. "But now we're missing one. And
I didn't take it!"

Mom and Dad got out of the water. They walked over to where Shawna
was standing. They looked under the towels and under the picnic blanket,
but they couldn't find the missing lunch bag. Suddenly they heard a
scream from behind them. It was Keesha, Shawna's little sister.

"It's leaping! Look! The lunch bag is leaping!" Keesha exclaimed.

Mom, Dad, and Shawna turned to see where Keesha was pointing.
They saw a brown paper bag moving across the sand in short, jerky
motions. Just then, it stopped moving, and a pink claw poked out.

Mom started laughing, and everyone else joined in. "Well, next time
we'll have to pack our lunches in a cooler," Mom said.

"Yeah," said Shawna. "Otherwise we'll have to pack an extra lunch for
the crab!"

Use with page 49.

Lesson 11

Practice: Using Text Evidence

Directions: Use "The Leaping Lunch Bag" to answer the
following questions.

1. How did Shawna's sister, Keesha, react when she saw the "leaping lunch bag"?

_____

_____

Explain ▶ *Write the evidence from the passage that supports your answer.*

_____

_____

2. What was causing the paper bag to move across the sand?

   (A) A squirrel was taking it to its nest.

   (C) Shawna had tied it to a string to tease Keesha.

   (B) A seagull had picked it up in its beak.

   (D) A sand crab was in the bag.

Explain ▶ *Write the evidence from the passage that supports your answer.*

_____

_____

3. What do you think Shawna and her family learned from this incident?

_____

_____

Explain ▶ *Write the evidence from the passage that supports your answer.*

_____

_____

✓ CHECK Did you find evidence in the passages to support each of your answers?

Use with page 48.

Lesson 12

Justifying and Checking Your Answer

STUDENT OBJECTIVES

- Justify and check answers to questions about a passage.

Resources

- Passage 12, page 51
- Practice 12, page 52

Tip for Success

Remember, a successful test taker does not become stressed about the test.

Teach/Model

Introduce Remind students that any answer they choose or write must be justified by the passage. When they answer a *literal question,* which asks for information that is directly stated in the passage, they should check back in the passage to be certain that the text matches their answer.

Tell students that even if they think they can recall the answer as they read a question, they should still take a quick look at the passage to make sure that answer is correct. If the passage justifies, or confirms, the answer, they can write the answer confidently and move on. If students cannot recall the answer immediately, they should look in the passage for key words from the question.

Preview Look at the **Passage** and **Practice, pages 51–52,** with students. Read the directions aloud.

Read the passage aloud while students follow along.

> **THINK ALOUD** *Now I will start on the questions. I will make sure that every answer I choose or write is justified by the passage.*

QUESTION 1 Read the question aloud. Model the thinking process students might use to answer the question.

> **THINK ALOUD** *I believe I read that inventors in Scotland added pedals to help turn the wheels. But before writing, I will look to make sure that the passage justifies my answer. Spotting the word* Scotland, *I find that the second sentence in the third paragraph confirms my answer. So I will restate the question and complete the statement as: "Scottish inventors added pedals to the bicycle to make it easier to use."*

Guided Practice

Have students complete **questions 2** and **3.** When students finish, encourage them to share their work with the group.

Check Progress Refer to **Answer Key, page 147.**

(Lesson 12)

Directions: Read the following passage. Then answer
questions 1 through 3.

The Story of Bicycles

What is better than pedaling your bike down the street on a beautiful
day? People have been enjoying bike rides for hundreds of years.

The first bicycle was made in France in 1690. It didn't look anything
like the sleek, speedy bikes we ride today. It was made up of two wheels
connected by a bar. It had no handlebars and no pedals. The rider had to
make this bicycle go by pushing his or her feet against the ground. About
126 years later, a German inventor added a handlebar to the front of his
bicycle. The handlebar allowed him to turn the front wheel and control
where the bicycle went. But he still had to push the bike along with
his feet.

By 1839, bicycles started to look more like the ones we use today.
Inventors in Scotland added pedals to help turn the wheels of the bicycle.
Then a French inventor built a bicycle with a front wheel that was slightly
larger than the back wheel. In 1873, an English inventor named James
Starley made the front wheel three times as big as the back wheel. That
style of bicycle is often pictured in encyclopedias.

Finally, in 1880, inventors made a safer bicycle that was closer to the
ground. That was the bicycle that became popular in the United States.

Today's bicycles have come a long way from the early models. Racing
or touring bikes are very light and allow the rider to move quickly.
Mountain bikes have thick wheels and sturdy frames. These features help
make the ride smoother on rocky ground.

Bikes have always had one thing in common. They have always given
people a quick, enjoyable way to get from one place to another.

Use with page 52.

(Lesson 12)

Practice: Justifying and Checking Your Answer

Directions: Use "The Story of Bicycles" to answer the following questions.

1. What did Scottish inventors add to the bicycle to make it easier to use?

_____

_____

 Explain *Write the sentence from the passage that justifies your answer.*

_____

2. The bicycle invented in 1880 was safer than earlier models because _____.

(A) it was closer to the ground

(B) it had brakes

(C) it had a rearview mirror

(D) its front wheel was larger than its back wheel

Explain *Write the sentence from the passage that justifies your answer.*

_____

3. Why do today's mountain bikes ride smoothly on rocky ground?

_____

_____

Explain *Write the sentence from the passage that justifies your answer.*

_____

✓CHECK Can you justify each of your answers?

Use with page 51.

Lesson 13
Open-Ended Questions

Teach/Model

Introduce Explain that some test questions require students to write a short response to a question or statement. Responses must be based on an accompanying passage or graphic. Students should use details and information from the passage to support their ideas. Point out that they can sometimes use the space provided as a rough guide to the amount of detail expected, but often the allotted space is the same for every question, regardless of the answer expected.

Discuss the following strategies for answering short-response questions, referring students to previous lessons as needed:

- Before you read the passage, preview the questions and identify what they are asking. **(Lesson 4)** You may need to restate the question in your own words.

- Determine whether the answer to the question is in the text or "in my head." **(Lesson 6)**

- Check the passage for information and details to support your response. **(Lesson 11)**

- Rehearse your answer informally in your head before writing.

- To answer some open-ended questions, it is a good strategy to begin by restating the question as a statement that can be completed. **(Lesson 3)**

- Take about five minutes. Use your time to make sure that your response is accurate and that it answers every part of the question.

- Be sure to use complete sentences and correct spelling, grammar, and punctuation.

Preview Look at the **Passage** and **Practice, pages 54–55,** with students. Read the directions aloud.

> **THINK ALOUD** *Before I read, I will preview the questions so that I can look for the information as I read. These are not multiple-choice questions. I have to write the answers in complete sentences.*

Read the passage aloud while students follow along.

Question 1 Read the question aloud. Model how to think about the question.

> **THINK ALOUD** *First, I will restate the question: "The editorial says that Ms. Gonsalves does have enough experience." The next-to-last paragraph contains the facts and details used for support. I will write, "She has participated in Beachview government as a member of the City Council, and she is president of the Chamber of Commerce." When I give my own opinion for question 3, I will support it like this with facts.*

Guided Practice

Have students complete **questions 2** and **3.** Encourage them to share their work .

Check Progress Refer to **Answer Key, page 147.**

STUDENT OBJECTIVES
- Write short answers to open-ended questions.

Resources
- Passage 13, page 54
- Practice 13, page 55

Tip for Success

Remember, a successful test taker looks for cue words in the question.

Lesson 13

Directions: Read the following passage. Then answer questions 1 through 3.

Marisa Gonsalves for Mayor

After careful consideration, the Beachview Times-Tribune has decided to endorse City Council member Marisa Gonsalves for mayor of Beachview.

Rosa de Carlo, the current mayor, who is Ms. Gonsalves's opponent, has done many good things for Beachview. Her expansion of the city hospital was a long-needed improvement. But going forward, we think that the city would be better off with Ms. Gonsalves as mayor.

First, we believe that Ms. Gonsalves has a better vision for the future. She is prepared to make meaningful changes to solve the biggest problem currently facing Beachview: the massive traffic tie-ups we frequently experience downtown. Her solution—a wise one, we feel—is to appoint a commission of business people and city planners to recommend an all-new traffic plan for downtown.

Mayor de Carlo, on the other hand, would merely add more traffic lights. And to pay for them, she suggests installing parking meters. Ms. Gonsalves argues—and we agree—that more traffic lights will only make the congestion worse.

Second, we think that the city is weary of Mayor de Carlo's confrontational style. Clearly, Ms. Gonsalves's more conciliatory manner would be a welcome change. Ms. de Carlo's stubbornness has alienated many Council members, who are now unwilling to work with her or to support her programs. Ms. Gonsalves, on the other hand, has shown that she knows how to use soothing words to appeal to friends and opponents alike. Her agreeable, easygoing style is just what Beachview needs now.

Finally, we reject Mayor de Carlo's argument that Ms. Gonsalves lacks the experience to be mayor. As a member of the City Council, Ms. Gonsalves has become intimately familiar with the workings of the Beachview government. She is also currently the president of our Chamber of Commerce. In that job, which is as difficult as being mayor, she has shown herself to be a gifted administrator.

The Beachview Times-Tribune urges you to vote for Marisa Gonsalves for mayor.

Use with page 55.

(Lesson 13)

Practice: Open-Ended Questions

Directions: Use "Marisa Gonsalves for Mayor" to answer the following questions.

1. What does the editorial say about Mayor de Carlo's statement that Ms. Gonsalves does not have the experience to be mayor?

_____

Explain ▶ *What facts and details support this statement?*

_____

_____

2. How does the editorial compare and contrast Ms. Gonsalves's and Mayor de Carlo's way of dealing with the City Council?

_____

Explain ▶ *What similar and different details does the editorial give about each candidate?*

_____

_____

_____

3. In your opinion, who offers a better plan for traffic control? Use specific information from the editorial and your own reasoning to support your answer.

_____

_____

_____

✓CHECK Did you use complete sentences?

Use with page 54.

Lesson 14

Using Test Time Effectively

STUDENT OBJECTIVES

- Manage time for effective pacing during test-taking.

Resources

- Practice 14, page 57

Tip for Success

Remember, a successful test taker makes educated guesses when some multiple-choice options can be eliminated.

Teach/Model

Introduce Explain that good test scores require more than possessing the skills and knowledge that are tested. Test takers also need to answer as many questions as possible before time runs out.

> **THINK ALOUD** *When I'm planning for a test, I know I need to find out how much time will be allowed. How many questions of each type will there be?*

Find information about upcoming tests your students will be taking, and model strategies for pacing and managing time. For example, if 40 multiple-choice questions are to be answered in 30 minutes, then you need to plan on an average of 45 seconds per question. If a multiple-choice question is worth 5 points and a short-answer question is worth 20, allow more time for the short-answer question.

Present the following strategies for managing time effectively:

- Decide how much time, on average, you should spend on each type of question.

- If a question is taking you too long, skip it and return to it later. Be sure to leave a space on your answer sheet for the skipped question.

- When you return to a skipped question, try to eliminate choices you know are incorrect. If you don't know, guess smart. If wrong answers do not count against you, or if you can eliminate one or more answer choices, guess at the answer.

- If time runs out and you know you will not be able to finish an essay, short-answer, or extended-response question, try to write a short outline of any you have not finished. Sometimes you can get partial credit.

- As you practice taking tests, become aware of your test-taking and time-management habits. Then you can set goals for improvement.

Look at **Trackers 1** and **2** on **page 57** with students. Read the directions aloud.

> **THINK ALOUD** *On Tracker 1, I will write down the time I start and finish each type of question. This will help me set goals for improved time management. For example, I should spend about 5 minutes on a short-answer question with 8 write-on lines, and about 10 minutes on an extended-response question with 14 write-on lines. I use Tracker 2 the same way. When I have a writing prompt for an essay question, I may have about 45 minutes to write a 5-paragraph essay.*

Guided Practice

Have students use the trackers as they work through practice tests. After each test, encourage them to compare notes with classmates.

Check Progress Check students' tracking sheets after each practice test.

Lesson 14

Practice: Using Test Time Effectively

Tracker 1: Reading and Writing Questions

Directions: Write the start and finish times for each section of the test. Then figure out the number of minutes you spent.

Date: _____

	Time Started	Time Finished	Minutes Spent
Multiple Choice			
Short Answer			
Extended Response			

It took me _____ minutes to complete _____ multiple-choice questions.

It took me _____ minutes to complete _____ short-answer questions.

It took me _____ minutes to complete _____ extended responses.

I should spend (more/less) time on _____ .

Tracker 2: Essay Questions

Directions: Write your start and finish times for each step. Then figure out the number of minutes you spent on each step.

Date: _____

	Time Started	Time Finished	Minutes Spent
Plan			
Draft			
Check/Proofread			

It took me _____ minutes to complete my planning page.

It took me _____ minutes to write the draft of my essay.

It took me _____ minutes to check and proofread my essay.

I should spend (more/less) time on _____ .

Use with page 56.

Lesson 15

Identifying Narrative Prompts

STUDENT OBJECTIVES

- Identify narrative writing prompts.

Resources

- Practice 15, page 59

Tip for Success

Remember, a successful test taker brings sharpened pencils for the test.

Teach/Model

Introduce Explain that a *narrative* tells a story. It can be a real-life story about something that happened to the writer, or it can be a fictional story with make-believe characters. Tell students that their stories or essays should have a clear *beginning, middle,* and *end.* At the beginning of the story, students should identify the *characters, setting,* and *plot.* The middle should describe the action that took place. The end of the story should bring the events to a conclusion. Encourage students to add other details about narrative writing. *(They may share that a narrative is usually written in the first person.)*

Point out to students that a *narrative writing prompt* generally asks you to write a story or essay about yourself. Explain that a narrative writing prompt will have key words that help to identify it. For example, they might see the words: *tell about a time; tell what happened; write a story about.*

Preview Look at **Practice, page 59.** Read the directions aloud.

> **THINK ALOUD** *As I read the prompts, I will look for key words that tell me what type of prompt it is.*

Read aloud the writing prompt with students following along. Then model the process students might use to identify the type of prompt.

> **THINK ALOUD** *I see these words in the last paragraph of the prompt:* Write an essay telling about a time. *I know that these key words make it clear that the prompt is a narrative writing prompt. I will underline these words.*

QUESTION 1 Read the question aloud. Model the process students might use to answer the question.

> **THINK ALOUD** *The question asks which words in the prompt signal that it is a narrative writing prompt. I have underlined:* Write an essay telling about a time. *So I will write these words on the line provided.*

QUESTION 2 Read the next question aloud.

> **THINK ALOUD** *Because this is a narrative writing prompt, I know that the response a test grader would expect is a story telling about a time when I experienced the power of nature. The action in the story must give a sense of what happened first, next, and last. It must focus on the events that made the experience something to remember.*

Guided Practice

Have students read **Writing Prompt 2** and follow the directions for answering **questions 3** and **4.** When students finish, encourage them to share their work with the group.

Check Progress Refer to **Answer Key, page 147.**

Lesson 15

Practice: Identifying Narrative Prompts

Directions: Read each prompt. Underline the key words that tell you what kind of prompt it is. Then answer questions 1 through 4.

Writing Prompt 1

Nature can be a powerful force! Think about an experience you had that made you stop and take notice of nature's power.

Before you write, think about that time. Where were you? What happened that made you remember the experience?

Write an essay telling about a time when you were amazed by nature.

1. Which words in the prompt let you know that it is a narrative writing prompt?

_____

2. What would a test grader expect to find in an essay response to this narrative writing prompt?

_____

_____

_____

Writing Prompt 2

Imagine that you are living in the year 3000. What would your typical day be like?

Before you write, think about the way things might be different. How would people get around? How would they communicate? What type of clothes would they wear?

Write an essay telling about a day in your life in the year 3000.

3. Which words in the prompt let you know that it is a narrative writing prompt?

_____

4. What would a test grader expect to find in an essay response to this narrative writing prompt?

_____

_____

_____

✓**CHECK** Did you find the key words that help you identify the prompt as a narrative writing prompt?

Use with page 58.

Lesson 16

Identifying Expository Prompts

STUDENT OBJECTIVES

• Identify expository writing prompts.

Resources

• Practice 16, page 61

Tip for Success

Remember, a successful test taker doesn't begin studying on the night before a test.

Teach/Model

Introduce Explain to students that *expository writing* is writing that gives factual information. It may explain how something works or why something happens. It may also describe the steps in a process or tell how to do or make something. Expository writing is often written in sequential order using words such as *first, second,* and *finally.*

Ask students what else they know about expository writing. *(They may share the idea that all forms of expository writing are types of nonfiction. They may also add that it is like the writing in their science and social studies textbooks.)*

Point out that on tests an *expository writing prompt* is one that asks for writing that provides information. Explain that the way to identify an expository writing prompt is to look for these key words or phrases: *define, explain how, explain why,* or *tell what steps to take.* Tell students that the direction line will ask them to write an essay. Remind students that the essay is expected to be in a five-paragraph format.

Preview Look at **Practice, page 61.** Read the directions aloud.

> **THINK ALOUD** *As I read the prompt, I will look for the key words that tell me what type of prompt this is.*

Read the prompt aloud while students follow along. Then model the process students might use to identify what type of writing the prompt asks them to do.

> **THINK ALOUD** *In the last paragraph of the prompt, I see these key words:* write an essay *and* explain how. *I know that these are the key words that signal an expository prompt.*

QUESTION 1 Read the question aloud. Model the process students might use to answer the question.

> **THINK ALOUD** *The question asks which words in the prompt make it clear that this is an expository writing prompt. I will underline:* write an essay *and* explain how. *Then, I will write these words on the line.*

QUESTION 2 Read the question aloud. Model the process this question requires.

> **THINK ALOUD** *Because I know that this is an expository writing prompt, I know that the response a test grader expects is an essay about an object that someone from another planet might not recognize and/or know how to use. I need to make sure that I explain clearly what the object looks like and how it is used.*

Guided Practice

Have students read **Writing Prompt 2** and follow the directions for answering **questions 3** and **4.** When students finish, encourage them to share their work with the group.

Check Progress Refer to **Answer Key, page 147.**

(Lesson 16)

Practice: Identifying Expository Prompts

Directions: Read each prompt. Underline the key words that let you know the kind of prompt it is. Then answer questions 1 through 4.

Writing Prompt 1

Suppose you were an exchange student going to school on another planet. You want to explain how an object unfamiliar to your classmates is used on Earth.

Before you write, think about the object you have chosen. What does it look like? How is it used?

Write an essay for your new schoolmates to explain how people on Earth use the object.

1. Which words or phrases in the prompt make it clear that it is an expository writing prompt?

_____

2. What would a test grader expect to find in an essay response to this expository writing prompt?

_____

_____

_____

Writing Prompt 2

Suppose you have a new neighbor. There is a sport that you like to play, but your new friend has never played it. You want to tell your friend how to play the sport.

Before you write, think about the sport. What is the object? What are the rules? How does a team win?

Write an essay to explain how to play the sport.

3. Which words or phrases let you know that it is an expository writing prompt?

_____

4. What would a test grader expect to find in an essay response to this expository writing prompt?

_____

_____

_____

✓**CHECK** Did you look for and underline key words in the prompt that help you to identify an expository writing prompt?

Use with page 60.

Identifying Persuasive Prompts

STUDENT OBJECTIVES

- Identify persuasive writing prompts.

Resources

- Practice 17, page 63

Tip for Success

Remember, a successful test taker writes neatly.

Teach/Model

Introduce Explain that in *persuasive writing*, the writer tries to convince the reader to agree with a specific point of view or to take a specific action about an issue. Persuasive writing follows a definite plan. The writer presents his or her personal opinion, offers reasons to support it, and then summarizes his or her viewpoint.

Help students to understand that persuasive writing always presents solid reasons to support the opinions expressed. Supporting reasons can include facts, statistics, details, examples, or detailed explanations.

Ask students to think of examples of persuasive writing. *(They might share such examples as letters to the editor, political speeches, and even advertisements.)*

Explain that on tests a *persuasive writing prompt* is one that asks for the writing to have a clearly stated opinion and reasons to support it. Explain that the way to identify a persuasive writing prompt is to look for key words such as *convince, persuade, state your opinion, make a case,* or *give reasons for* in the prompt. Remind students that the essay is expected to be in a five-paragraph format.

Preview Look at **Practice, page 63,** with students. Read the directions aloud.

> **THINK ALOUD** *As I read Writing Prompt 1, I will look for key words that let me know what kind of prompt it is.*

Read aloud the prompt while students follow along. Then model the process students should use to identify the type of prompt.

QUESTION 1 Read the question aloud. Model the process students might use to answer the question.

> **THINK ALOUD** *In the last paragraph of the prompt, I see the words* convince *and* opinion. *I know that these key words indicate that it is a persuasive writing prompt. I will underline these words.*

QUESTION 2 Read the next question aloud. Model the process that this question requires.

> **THINK ALOUD** *Because this is a persuasive writing prompt, I know the test grader expects an essay that convinces my class to choose my suggestion for the field trip. The essay must begin by stating my opinion. It must offer reasons that support that opinion. In the conclusion, my viewpoint must be summarized.*

Guided Practice

Have students read **Writing Prompt 2** and follow the directions for answering **questions 3** and **4.** When students finish, encourage them to share their work with the group.

Check Progress Refer to **Answer Key, page 147.**

(Lesson 17)

Practice: Identifying Persuasive Prompts

Directions: Read each prompt. Underline the key words that tell you what kind of prompt it is. Then answer questions 1 through 4.

Writing Prompt 1

Your class is planning a field trip for the end of the school year. Each student is to submit an essay about where he or she thinks the class should go.

Before you write, decide on your choice for a place for the field trip. Write down a few reasons why your idea is a good one. What are some facts or examples that might support your choice?

Write an essay to convince your class why your opinion about the class field trip is a good one.

1. What words or phrases let you know that you are being asked to do persuasive writing?

_____

2. What would a test grader expect to find in an essay response to this persuasive writing prompt?

_____

_____

_____

_____

Writing Prompt 2

Suppose your school is considering introducing a dress code.

Before you write, think about how you feel about clothes and personal style. List reasons to support your view.

Write an essay to persuade school officials to agree with your position on a dress code.

3. What words or phrases let you know that you are being asked to do persuasive writing?

_____

4. What would a test grader expect to find in an essay response to this persuasive writing prompt?

_____

_____

_____

✓**CHECK** Did you underline the words in the prompt that help you identify a persuasive writing prompt?

Use with page 62.

Lesson 18

Restating the Prompt

STUDENT OBJECTIVES

- Restate a writing prompt in an introductory sentence to begin an essay.

Resources

- Practice 18, page 65

Tip for Success

Remember, a successful test taker always gets a good night's sleep the night before the test.

Teach/Model

Introduce Remind students that a writing prompt presents a topic to write about and tells what kind of writing is expected. Most prompts offer several ideas to help students get started. Explain that students can identify suggestions because they use phrases such as *before you write* or *think about.*

Remind students to read a prompt looking for the key words about the topic and for words such as *tell, explain, convince,* or *persuade* that signal the kind of writing to do.

Explain to students that restating the prompt in the first, or introductory, sentence is a good way to make the topic clear to the reader. Tell students to repeat key words from the prompt in this introductory sentence.

Have students practice restating questions by using complete sentences to respond to simple questions you ask. (For example, *When is your birthday? My birthday is on . . .*)

Preview Look at **Practice, page 65,** with students. Read the directions aloud.

> **THINK ALOUD** *I know that I am expected to restate the prompt.*

Read aloud the writing prompt while students follow along. Model the process students might use to identify the type of writing and the topic of the essay.

> **THINK ALOUD** *I have read the prompt and I can see that the topic is* meeting a challenge. *The key words about the topic are* facing a challenge. *The key words* write an essay telling about *alert me that the kind of writing required is a narrative.*

QUESTION 1 Read the question aloud while students follow along. Model the process students might use to restate the prompt.

> **THINK ALOUD** *In my introductory sentence I can restate the prompt and say what challenge I faced. Because the topic is about me, I'll use an* I *statement.* "A challenge that I faced was . . ."

Write the beginning of your introductory sentence on the board. Read it aloud as students follow along. Invite students to suggest ideas to complete the sentence.

QUESTION 2 Read the next question aloud. Model the process this question requires.

> **THINK ALOUD** *Now I'll reread my introductory sentence to make sure it includes the key words in the prompt that relate to the topic.*

Guided Practice

Have students read **Writing Prompt 2** and follow the directions for answering **questions 3** and **4.** When students finish, encourage them to share their introductory sentences with the group.

Check Progress Refer to **Answer Key, page 147.**

(Lesson 18)

Practice: Restating the Prompt

Directions: Read each prompt. Then restate the prompt as the introductory sentence of an essay. You do not need to write the complete essay.

Writing Prompt 1

Everyone faces challenges in life.

Before you write, think about a challenge you have faced. What kind of challenge did you face? What happened?

Write an essay that tells about a challenge that you faced.

1. Restate the prompt for your introductory sentence.

_____

_____

2. What are the key words in your introductory sentence?

_____

Writing Prompt 2

Standing up for what you think is right can take a lot of courage.

Think about someone who stuck to his or her beliefs in the face of opposition. What beliefs did that person stand up for? What opposition did the person face?

Write an essay explaining how someone showed courage in standing up for his or her beliefs. Give specific details.

3. Restate the prompt for your introductory sentence.

_____

_____

4. What are the key words in your introductory sentence?

_____

✓**CHECK** Does your introductory sentence tell what the prompt wants you to write about?

Use with page 64.

Lesson 19

Generating Your Thoughts

STUDENT OBJECTIVES

- Generate thoughts by making quick notes and idea webs.

Resources

- Practice 19, page 67
- Idea Web, page 138

Tip for Success

Remember, a successful test taker always takes time to plan before beginning to write.

Teach/Model

Introduce Remind students that the prompt will provide the topic they must write about. Before they write, students will need to brainstorm, or generate, specific subjects related to the topic and then select one as the basis for their essay. Next, they will make quick notes about the subject that they have chosen.

Distribute copies of the **Idea Web, page 138,** to students. You may wish to put the web on a transparency. Tell them that they will use the web to organize their thoughts and notes in preparation for writing. Have students write the general essay topic on the line provided in the center circle. Then they will use the surrounding circles to write details that relate to the subject or support that main idea.

Preview Look at **Practice, page 67.** Read the directions aloud.

> **THINK ALOUD** *I know that on a test I will need to think quickly. I cannot spend a lot of time generating my thoughts during a test.*

Writing Prompt 1 Read Writing Prompt 1 aloud while the students follow along. Model the process students might use to narrow the topic.

> **THINK ALOUD** *This prompt tells me that the type of writing I am expected to do is an expository essay and the topic is a skill I've learned this year that will be important to me as an adult. Before I start to write, I need to think about what skills I have learned and choose one to write about. I've learned some new math skills and research skills in science, but the most important thing I learned so far this year is how to debate. I'll write about that.*

Notes Now model the process students might use to jot down their thoughts in quick notes.

> **THINK ALOUD** *I should jot down my thoughts about how debating will help me in the future. Debating will help me: organize my thoughts better; express and support a point of view when talking to friends or other adults; and succeed at jobs that require public speaking skills.*

Idea Web Model the process students might use to organize their thoughts in an idea web.

> **THINK ALOUD** *In the center box, I'll write the name of my subject:* how debating skills will help me. *I'll use the surrounding circles to organize the details I listed in my notes.*

Guided Practice

Distribute the **Idea Web** on **page 145** to students for use with this practice activity. Have students follow the same process with **Writing Prompt 2.** When students finish, encourage them to share their notes and webs with the group.

Check Progress Refer to **Answer Key, page 147.**

(Lesson 19)
Practice: Generating Your Thoughts

Directions: Read each prompt. Then generate your thoughts for an essay by jotting down quick notes. Use an idea web to organize your thoughts.

Writing Prompt 1

What is the one skill you have learned this year in school that you think will be most important to you as an adult?

Before you write your answer, think of the new skills you have learned and choose one to write about. What is the skill? How will you use this skill as an adult? Is it a job skill? Is it an everyday skill?

Write an essay explaining why the skill you chose will help you as an adult.

1. Jot down your thoughts in quick notes.

_____

_____

_____

_____

Now organize your thoughts using an idea web.

Writing Prompt 2

Your school has always offered many elective classes. Next year, because of budget cuts, they may be forced to cut some of these classes.

Think about what your opinion is on this issue. Before you write, think of three reasons that support your opinion.

Write an essay to convince the Board of Education to agree with your opinion on the issue of cutting elective classes from the schedule.

2. Jot down your thoughts in quick notes.

_____

_____

_____

_____

Now organize your thoughts using an idea web.

✓CHECK Did you put your subject in the center of the circle of your idea web and add supporting details around it?

Use with page 66.

Creating an Outline

STUDENT OBJECTIVES

- Create outlines from quick notes.

Resources

- Practice 20, page 69
- Outline Graphic Organizer, page 139

Tip for Success

Remember, a successful test taker reads over his or her essay before turning it in.

Teach/Model

Introduce Remind students that they have used their notes to make idea webs that help them to identify main ideas and supporting details. Explain that they may put those notes into an outline. The outline can help them plan a well-organized essay.

Tell students that making a five-part outline is the best way to organize an essay. Demonstrate how to make an outline by writing a main heading and at least two subheadings for the introductory paragraph.

I. You learn many things in science class.
  A. You learn about space.
  B. You learn the Periodic Table.

Explain to students that each main heading gives the main idea of a paragraph and that each subheading gives a supporting detail. Distribute copies of the **Outline Graphic Organizer, page 139.** You may wish to make a transparency of the graphic.

Preview Look at **Practice, page 69.** Read the directions aloud.

THINK ALOUD *Making an outline is sort of like making a checklist for your essay. It provides an order for your thoughts.*

Writing Prompt 1 Read the prompt aloud. Model how to choose a subject.

THINK ALOUD *The prompt tells me that the topic is a vacation to Hawaii or the Grand Canyon. Before I write, I need to decide which of the two vacations I would like better. I would rather go to the Grand Canyon so I will choose that as my topic.*

Notes Now model how students might make a few quick notes.

THINK ALOUD *Now I'll jot down reasons why the Grand Canyon appeals to me.*

- *one of America's great natural wonders*
- *can take a rafting trip on the Colorado River*
- *can hike the trails in the Canyon*
- *can see the color and beauty of the Canyon*

Outline Finally, model the process students might use to create an outline.

THINK ALOUD *Roman numeral I is for my Introduction. From my notes, I'll choose three main ideas to write about. On the blank outline, I'll write my main ideas in order next to the Roman numerals II–IV and my supporting details next to the letters A and B. Roman numeral V is for my conclusion.*

You may wish to complete an outline for the prompt. Encourage students to help.

Guided Practice

Have students follow the same process with **Writing Prompt 2.** When they finish, have them share their outlines with the group.

Check Progress Refer to **Answer Key, page 147.**

Lesson 20

Practice: Creating an Outline

Directions: Read each prompt. Then generate thoughts for an essay by jotting down quick notes. Create an outline to organize your essay.

Writing Prompt 1

You have just won a contest. Your choice is one of two vacations–learning how to scuba dive in Hawaii or camping in the Grand Canyon. Which one will you choose? Why?

Before you write your answer, choose the vacation that most appeals to you. Think of reasons why that vacation is the one for you.

Write an essay explaining why you would choose this particular vacation.

1. Jot down your thoughts in quick notes.

_____
_____
_____
_____

Now create an outline to organize your essay.

Writing Prompt 2

Everyone has a schoolteacher that they will always remember.

Before you write, think about all of the teachers you have had that you remember for one reason or another. Choose one. When did you have this teacher? What did this teacher do for you?

Write an essay telling about your experience with this teacher.

2. Jot down your thoughts in quick notes.

_____
_____
_____
_____

Now create an outline to organize your essay.

✓CHECK Did you write your main headings by the Roman numerals in your outline? Did your write your subheadings by the letters?

Use with page 68.

Lesson 21

Understanding Evaluation Criteria

STUDENT OBJECTIVES

- Identify criteria used to evaluate written responses, and revise writing to improve it.

Resources

- Passage 21, page 71
- Practice 21, page 72

Tip for Success

Remember, a successful test taker uses examples and details to make writing interesting.

Teach/Model

Introduce Remind students that they have now learned to identify narrative, expository, and persuasive writing prompts by using the strategy of finding the key words in the prompt. These key words let them know which kind of writing they are expected to do.

Explain that when they write an essay on a test, their essay is usually evaluated, or graded, by one or more readers. Each reader gives the writing a score. If there is more than one reader, then the average of the scores is taken to get a final score.

Evaluators, or readers, use *rubrics* to help them score the writing. Rubrics are a list of *criteria,* or things the evaluators look for in the writing in order to score it. For example, in a 6-point writing rubric, a 6 is the highest score and a 1 is the lowest. A 6-point paper will have everything listed in the criteria for that score. A 3-point paper may have some of the things the 6-point paper has, but there are things the writer could do to improve the score. (In a 4-point rubric, 4 is the highest score and 1 is the lowest. See **pages 132–135** for examples of scoring rubrics.)

Preview Look at the **Passage** and **Practice, pages 71–72.** Read the directions aloud. Then read the passage aloud while students follow along. Model the process students might use to understand how the essay might be evaluated.

THINK ALOUD *The essay responds directly to the prompt. There is an introduction, three paragraphs that explain, and a conclusion. The sentences are complete. But some of the words aren't very interesting. Some of the sentences could be changed to make this more interesting to read.*

QUESTION 1 Read the question aloud. Model the process students might use to answer the question.

THINK ALOUD *Even though the first sentence tells what the essay is about, it doesn't capture my attention. I can make it more interesting if I change the statement into a question like this:* Have you ever seen a rubber band before? *A question is better because it draws the reader in.*

QUESTION 2 Read the question aloud and model the process this question requires.

THINK ALOUD *The underlined words in the sentence,* gets longer, *don't really describe rubber very well. What's another word I could use instead? How about* stretches? *That's a better description of what rubber does. I'll rewrite the sentence:* Rubber stretches when you pull on it.

Guided Practice

Have students repeat the process with **questions 3** through **5.** When students finish, invite them to share their work with the group. Students may rewrite the essay using the changes made on the practice activity. See **page 144** for a writing test form.

Check Progress Refer to **Answer Key, page 147.**

Name _____

(Lesson 21)

Practice: Evaluation Criteria

Directions: Here is an example of a *Score 3* expository essay. Read the prompt. Next, read the passage. Then answer questions 1 through 5.

Prompt

Things that seem ordinary to us might be very unusual to someone living on another planet. Imagine that you are an exchange student going to school on another planet.

Before you write, think of an object that is part of everyday life on Earth, but which people on the other planet might never have seen.

Write an essay explaining what this object is and why it is used for your new friends.

Score 3

A Rubber Band

This is a rubber band. On Earth, we use rubber bands for many different things. It is quite a helpful object.

A rubber band is made from rubber, which comes from rubber trees. Rubber gets longer when you pull on it. When you let go, it goes back to its normal size.

A rubber band can be used to hold a bunch of things together, such as sticks or pens. It can also be used to tie your hair back into a ponytail. Potato chips stay fresher if you use a rubber band to tie the bag closed.

Rubber bands come in all kinds of sizes. Rubber bands come in all kinds of colors. Big rubber bands are useful for holding together large things because they're usually stronger. Little rubber bands are useful because they can fit in small spaces.

We use rubber bands all the time on Earth. They are a good invention.

Use with page 72.

(Lesson 21)

Practice: Evaluation Criteria

Directions: Use "A Rubber Band" to answer the following questions.

1. How would you rewrite the first sentence to make it more interesting? Write your new first sentence.

_____

_____

2. In the second paragraph, replace the underlined words with another word, or words, that are more descriptive. Rewrite the sentence with your new word.

_____

_____

3. What sentence could you add to the beginning of the third paragraph to make it flow better? Rewrite your new sentence.

_____

_____

4. How could you combine the first two sentences in the fourth paragraph? Write your new sentence.

_____

_____

5. What's another word you could use for the underlined word <u>good</u> in the last paragraph? Write your new sentence.

_____

_____

✓**CHECK** Did each of your new sentences improve the way the passage reads?

Practice Tests

Two levels of reading passages help scaffold students and build success with increasingly difficult text.

Writing practice tests and prompts provide multiple opportunities for practice with the most widely assessed forms of writing to address diverse student needs.

Reading Practice Tests

Level A Tests

Test 1: Don't Touch the Bat! 74

Test 2: Not Just Any Lizard 76

Test 3: A Trip to the Space Center 78

Test 4: Eagle, Fly High! 80

Test 5: Dusting for Prints 82

Test 6: Point of View 84

Test 7: Soybeans 86

Level B Tests

Test 1: Tallgirl Saves the Day 88

Test 2: The Legend of Flying Horse Lake 92

Test 3: Bigfoot Hoax Revealed 96

Test 4: Breaking Barriers 98

Test 5: The Furious Storm 102

Test 6: Southbound on the Freeway 108

Test 7: "Remember Wounded Knee" 110

Writing Practice Tests

Narrative Writing

Test 1 116

Test 2 117

Test 3 118

Expository Writing

Test 1 119

Test 2 120

Test 3 121

Persuasive Writing

Test 1 122

Test 2 123

Test 3 124

Writing Prompts

Narrative Prompts 125

Expository Prompts 127

Persuasive Prompts 129

Directions: Read the following passage. Then answer questions 1 through 6.

Don't Touch the Bat!

Jarod had been having a rough time in school. He never seemed to get any grades above a C. But Jarod had other talents—he was a good singer, an excellent artist, and he was great with kids. In fact, Jarod had an after-school job as a counselor at the local recreation center. The kids thought Jarod was cool, and they'd always behave when he was around.

One day, as Jarod showed up for work, he found some of the kids crowded in a corner of the playground. He had failed a math test that day and was in a terrible mood.

"Hey, guys," he said. "What's up?"

"It's a bat! A real, live bat!" one of the kids shouted.

Jarod stepped through the crowd and looked at the ground.

"That's a bat all right," Jarod said. "Stand clear. I'll call the custodian."

"We want to adopt it," one kid said.

"Forget it," Jarod replied.

"Why not?" another kid asked.

"Because a bat on the ground in the daytime could be dangerous. Never touch a grounded bat. They can carry diseases, especially rabies, which makes you insane and then kills you in fits of violent convulsions. If you find a bat like this, it might be because it has rabies, and it could bite you and give you the disease. Know what the cure for rabies includes? Fifteen shots right into your stomach."

"Ouch!" one kid shouted. "No!" yelled another.

The kids followed Jarod inside to get help. They were all talking nervously and asking Jarod more questions. The math test crossed his mind a few times. But as he talked to the kids, he smiled to himself, because he really didn't feel so bad anymore.

Use with page 75.

GO ON ➡

Directions: Use "Don't Touch the Bat!" to answer the following questions.

1. In the following sentence, what does the word *grounded* mean?

   "Never touch a grounded bat."

   Ⓐ not allowed to go out

   Ⓑ solidly based

   Ⓒ lying on the land

   Ⓓ chased from its home

2. According to the passage, why might a bat be on the ground or out in the daytime?

   Ⓐ It could have rabies.

   Ⓑ It is feeling playful.

   Ⓒ It is chasing after insects.

   Ⓓ It is resting in the sun.

3. Jarod's reaction to the bat can be described as _____.

   Ⓐ slow

   Ⓑ unhelpful

   Ⓒ calm

   Ⓓ irrational

4. The kids thought Jarod was _____.

   Ⓐ cool

   Ⓑ weird

   Ⓒ mean

   Ⓓ obnoxious

5. At the end of the story, why was Jarod smiling to himself?

   Ⓐ No one had been hurt.

   Ⓑ He had gotten to see a bat up close.

   Ⓒ He didn't feel bad anymore.

   Ⓓ He was going to retake the test.

6. In the story, how does Jarod solve the problem of keeping the children safe?

   _____

   _____

   _____

   _____

   _____

STOP

Use with page 74.

Directions: Read the passage. Decide whether each underlined section contains an error. Then look at the answer choices on page 77. Find the answer that corrects the error. If there is no error, choose "No Mistake."

Not Just Any Lizard

Tania looked at the small, rather funny-looking creature <u>in front of</u>

<u>her She knew</u> that it was a lizard, but she <u>didn't know what kind. It</u> had a
    (1)   (2)

flattened head and a stumpy tail. Tania thought it <u>must have lost part of</u>

<u>its tale. Then</u> she decided it was supposed to look like that. The lizard
    (3)

was tan with bumpy <u>scales. It had tinny toes</u> spread far apart. Tania
                            (4)

<u>called to her dad. When him came</u> into the room, he laughed and <u>asked</u>
               (5)

<u>her, "where did you get that gecko?"</u>
            (6)

Use with page 77.

GO ON ➡

Directions: Select the answer that corrects each error in "Not Just Any Lizard."
If there is no error, choose "No Mistake."

1. Ⓐ in front of her She knowed

Ⓑ in front of her, She knew

Ⓒ in front of her. She knew

Ⓓ No Mistake

2. Ⓐ did'nt know what kind. It

Ⓑ didn't know what kind. it

Ⓒ didn't know what kind, it

Ⓓ No Mistake

3. Ⓐ must have lost part of its tale then

Ⓑ must have lost part of it's tale. Then

Ⓒ must have lost part of its tail. Then

Ⓓ No Mistake

4. Ⓐ scales. it had tinny toes

Ⓑ scales. It had tiny toes

Ⓒ scales. It had tiny tows

Ⓓ No Mistake

5. Ⓐ called to her dad. When he came

Ⓑ called to her dad, When him came

Ⓒ caled to her dad. When he came

Ⓓ No Mistake

6. Ⓐ asked her. "where did you get that gecko?"

Ⓑ asked her, "Wear did you get that gecko?"

Ⓒ asked her, "Where did you get that gecko?"

Ⓓ No Mistake

STOP

Use with page 76.

Directions: Read the following passage. Then answer
questions 1 through 6.

A Trip to the Space Center

"Look at this," Ramon said to his cousin Jacob and Jacob's mother,
Gloria, as they toured the Johnson Space Center. The Space Center is in
Houston, Texas. "That's the kind of space suit I will wear someday. I'm
going to be an astronaut. This will be my training center. What do you
want to do when you grow up, Jacob?"

"This astronaut stuff is cool," Jacob replied, "but I think I still want
to be a computer engineer. Are you ready to go to the rocket park?"

"Not yet," Ramon said. "I want to stay here a little longer. You haven't
taken my picture in the space suit yet."

Gloria, Ramon's aunt, laughed. Every year, Ramon wants his picture
taken in the space suit.

After a quick lunch, Gloria took the boys to see other exhibits. They
saw photos taken from outer space, moon rocks, and Mission Control.
They also learned about the history of space travel. Ramon knew that the
spacecraft he would blast off in someday would look much different.

After a while, Jacob's mom noticed that it was getting late. They had
spent almost the whole day at the Space Center.

"It's time to go, guys," Gloria said.

"Not yet, Gloria, please," Ramon said. "We haven't seen the film."

"Ramon," she said, "if you agree to leave right now, we can rent a
movie to watch tonight about astronauts and space travel. You probably
have the movie here memorized, anyway."

Ramon reluctantly agreed because he knew he would visit the Space
Center again next year.

Use with page 79.

GO ON ▶

Directions: Use "A Trip to the Space Center" to answer the following questions.

1. **Why didn't Ramon want to leave the Space Center in the late afternoon?**

   Ⓐ He and Jacob hadn't had lunch yet.

   Ⓑ He hadn't been to the rocket park yet.

   Ⓒ He and Jacob hadn't seen the space film yet.

   Ⓓ Gloria hadn't bought them any souvenirs yet.

2. **The phrase** *blast off* **means** _____.

   Ⓐ argue loudly

   Ⓑ take off

   Ⓒ blow up

   Ⓓ give a speech

3. **In the passage, Ramon tells Jacob and Gloria that he is** _____.

   Ⓐ more interested in computers than in space travel

   Ⓑ worried about going back to school

   Ⓒ going to become an astronaut someday

   Ⓓ not interested at all in space travel

4. **When did the boys see photos taken from outer space?**

   Ⓐ after lunch

   Ⓑ after the movie

   Ⓒ before lunch

   Ⓓ at the rocket park

5. **Which of the following is true about Ramon's visit to the Space Center?**

   Ⓐ It rained all day.

   Ⓑ Ramon did not see the film.

   Ⓒ The visit was finished by lunchtime.

   Ⓓ Ramon was visiting the Center all by himself.

6. **Why must Ramon's aunt persuade him to leave the Space Center?**

   _____

   _____

   _____

   _____

   _____

Use with page 78.

Directions: Read the following passage. Then answer questions 1 through 6.

Eagle, Fly High!

If Benjamin Franklin had had his way, the turkey would be our national bird. But as everyone knows, the bald eagle, not the turkey, holds this honor. However, by the 1960s this noble bird was in danger. Only 500 nesting pairs of bald eagles remained then. Scientists soon learned why.

Certain chemicals were being used to protect crops from insects. Small animals ate crops with these chemicals on them. Eagles ate these small animals. Those chemicals eventually affected the eagles' eggs. The shells of their eggs became very thin. Often the shells cracked before the young could develop. However, farmers have made changes in how they fertilize their crops and protect them from insects. These changes have turned the situation around. Now eagles can be seen all around the country.

One good place to see eagles in the winter is the South. Eagles like to spend the winter along riverbanks there. They catch and eat fish there. Boaters in Texas often see eagles' nests in the bare tree branches along the shore. The nests are up to four feet wide. The nests often have eggs in them. The eagle eggs hatch in the spring.

People sometimes don't realize that they have seen a bald eagle. There's a reason for that. An eagle doesn't develop its familiar great white-feathered hood until it is four years old.

The eagle's future is bright now. This means that people have a very good chance of seeing eagles and shouting, "Look over there! There's one!"

Use with page 81.

GO ON ➡

Name _____

Directions: Use "Eagle, Fly High!" to answer the following questions.

1. What did Benjamin Franklin suggest for the national bird?

   Ⓐ the eagle

   Ⓑ the turkey

   Ⓒ the pheasant

   Ⓓ the lark

2. In the following sentence, what does the word *bright* mean?

"The eagle's future is bright now."

   Ⓐ shining

   Ⓑ intelligent

   Ⓒ hopeful

   Ⓓ brilliantly colored

3. According to the passage, where do bald eagles like to spend the winter?

   Ⓐ beside the Caribbean Sea in Mexico

   Ⓑ high up in the Rocky Mountains

   Ⓒ along the banks of rivers in the South

   Ⓓ along the rocky California seacoast

4. Eagles' eggs hatch in the _____ .

   Ⓐ spring

   Ⓑ river

   Ⓒ fall

   Ⓓ winter

5. What happened after farmers made changes in how they fertilize their crops and protect them from insects?

   Ⓐ The eagle population decreased to only 500 nesting pairs.

   Ⓑ The eagle was made the national bird of the United States.

   Ⓒ The eagles stopped eating small animals.

   Ⓓ The eagle population increased.

6. What caused the shells of eagles' eggs to become thin and likely to crack?

_____

_____

_____

Use with page 80.

READ 180 Test-Taking Strategies   81

Directions: Read the following passage. Then answer questions 1 through 6.

Dusting for Prints

Did you know that every time you touch an object you leave something behind? You leave fingerprints. The skin on each of your fingertips has a pattern. Oils from your skin follow the pattern on your fingertip and leave behind a print of the pattern on anything you touch.

No two people have prints that are exactly the same. For this reason, detectives use fingerprints to help them solve crimes. After they take fingerprints, they can compare the prints with other prints that they have taken. They can match the prints up with those stored on police computer files.

You can perform a simple experiment to learn how to dust for fingerprints the way that police officers do. First, find an object with a hard, shiny surface. Use a clean cloth to wipe the surface of the object. In that way, you get rid of any old fingerprints. Now, pick up the object with one hand and then set it down. The object now has your fingerprints on it.

Next, use a clean, dry paintbrush to lightly dust some baby powder onto the object. Gently blow away most of the powder. Wherever there is a fingerprint, the powder will stick to the oils left from your fingertips. Use a magnifying glass to take a close look at the fingerprints.

While no two fingerprints are exactly the same, fingerprints follow common patterns. The diagram below shows some of these patterns.

 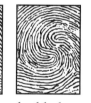   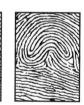

| loop | double loop | arch | pointed arch | whorl | mixed |

Use with page 83.

GO ON ▶

Directions: Use "Dusting for Prints" to answer the following questions.

1. In the following sentence from the passage, what does the word *gently* mean?

"**Gently blow away most of the powder.**"

Ⓐ in a gentle way

Ⓑ the opposite of gentle

Ⓒ a person who is gentle

Ⓓ less gentle

2. When you perform your fingerprint experiment, what is the first thing you should do?

Ⓐ Use a magnifying glass to look for fingerprints.

Ⓑ Wash your hands to remove any oils on them.

Ⓒ Find a hard, shiny object to use in the experiment.

Ⓓ Dust some baby powder on the object.

3. Fingerprints are left on objects because of _____.

Ⓐ dust

Ⓑ lotion

Ⓒ oil

Ⓓ soap

4. Which of the following is NOT a type of fingerprint pattern shown on the diagram?

Ⓐ pointed arch

Ⓑ double loop

Ⓒ single wave

Ⓓ whorl

5. An object that would NOT show fingerprints easily is a _____.

Ⓐ large mirror

Ⓑ bumpy, grainy leather wallet

Ⓒ hard plastic toy

Ⓓ juice glass

6. Based on the diagrams, what is the difference between the whorl fingerprint pattern and the arch pattern?

_____

_____

_____

_____

_____

Use with page 82.

Directions: Read the following poem. Then answer questions 1 through 6.

Point of View

by Virginia Larrain

Two kids were walking down the street,
One looking up, the other at her feet,
Both of them had known a similar life,
Living in a city of hope and strife.

The one with her eyes looking all around
Found only beauty in her big home town.
She saw flowers peeping out of the cracks,
She had friends who would never turn their backs.

The other looking down was quick to say,
"I can't see a thing but dirt and decay.
Look at the cracks in the wall over there.
What can I do? Why should I care?"

So the two grew up with their different views,
One looking up, the other at her shoes.
They both saw the city through different eyes,
And for that reason, led different lives.

The first was a dreamer, open and kind,
Glad for all the good things that she could find.
The second led a life filled with despair;
She saw the world as a burden to bear.

Use with page 85.

GO ON ➡

Directions: Use "Point of View" to answer the following questions.

1. Which of the following words from the poem describe the city as the second girl sees it?

Ⓐ "her big home town"

Ⓑ "dirt and decay"

Ⓒ "friends who would never turn their backs"

Ⓓ "all the good things that she could find"

2. In the following sentence from the poem, what do the words *through different eyes* mean?

"**They both saw the city through different eyes.**"

Ⓐ at separate times

Ⓑ through glasses

Ⓒ with different attitudes

Ⓓ in a make-believe way

3. The first girl was described by the poet as _____.

Ⓐ gentle

Ⓑ unhappy

Ⓒ open

Ⓓ naive

4. In the following line from the poem, what does the word *bear* mean?

"**She saw the world as a burden to bear.**"

Ⓐ bring forth

Ⓑ carry

Ⓒ uncover

Ⓓ give birth to

5. Which of the following best describes the author's purpose in writing the poem?

Ⓐ to contrast two different ways of looking at life

Ⓑ to compare two different parts of the city

Ⓒ to describe the uselessness of life in the city

Ⓓ to convince the reader not to live in a city

6. Which words in the poem help set the tone of the "other girl's" point of view? Give some examples.

_____

_____

_____

Use with page 84.

Directions: Read the following passage. Then answer questions 1 through 6.

Soybeans

Soybeans are plants that provide food for animals and people. They were one of the first crops raised by ancient peoples nearly 5,000 years ago. Today, farmers in the United States grow more soybeans than any other crop except for corn and wheat.

Soybeans are a very good source of vegetable protein. They are also inexpensive to produce. They cost much less than other protein sources such as meat, eggs, or cheese. As a result, soybeans are likely to play a growing role in nourishing the world's growing population. Around the world, many people cannot afford costly meat and dairy products. But they can grow and use soybeans instead. That way they will be able to get the protein they need.

Soybeans are used most often in the forms of soy meal and soy oil. Soy meal can be finely ground into soy flour. Soy flour is used in baby food, cereals, baked goods, and pet food. Soy oil is made into products such as edible refined oil. This oil is used to make margarine, cooking oil, mayonnaise, and salad dressings. The chart shows the food value of soybeans.

Food Value of Soybeans

Component	Percent of Total Food Value
Ash	4.7
Carbohydrates	33.5
Fat	17.7
Protein	34.1
Water	10

Use with page 87.

GO ON

Directions: Use "Soybeans" to answer the following questions.

1. If the word *expensive* means "costly," what does *inexpensive* mean?

Ⓐ very costly

Ⓑ free of cost

Ⓒ expensive but useful

Ⓓ not costly

2. According to the chart, water makes up what portion of soybeans' total food value?

Ⓐ 10 percent

Ⓑ 15 percent

Ⓒ 17 percent

Ⓓ 34 percent

3. Soybeans are a _____.

Ⓐ dairy product

Ⓑ vegetable

Ⓒ meat

Ⓓ grain

4. Soybeans can help nourish the world's growing population because _____.

Ⓐ they are an inexpensive source of protein

Ⓑ they can grow almost anywhere

Ⓒ the United States is the leading producer of soybeans

Ⓓ they are high in carbohydrates

5. Which of the following best expresses the main idea of this passage?

Ⓐ Farmers have raised soybeans for more than 5,000 years.

Ⓑ Soybeans are used to make soy meal and soy oil.

Ⓒ The soybean is a valuable yet inexpensive protein source with a wide variety of uses.

Ⓓ Farmers in the United States grow more soybeans than any other crop.

6. What products are made from soybeans?

_____

_____

_____

STOP

Use with page 86.

Directions: Read the story. Then answer questions 1 through 10.

Tallgirl Saves the Day

Tallulah did not have many friends at the 24th Street School, but she was not feeling particularly sociable anyway. Her closest friend, Alva, had moved to Worcester at the end of August and Tallulah, nicknamed Lu, really missed her. Now they kept in touch by telephone occasionally and by email almost every day.

On Thursday, school was a nightmare for Lu. First, she got into trouble for walking into homeroom late without an excuse. Next, she forgot to submit her homework in math class and got detention after school. Then, she lost her lunch money and had to sit in the cafeteria with a cup of tea, pretending that she was not hungry. Nothing seemed to be going right.

Lu sighed with relief when she finally got home to her apartment, even though her mom would not be home from work for another few hours. Lu didn't mind being alone for a while—at least no one could criticize her or tell her what to do.

After such a distressing day, Lu really wanted to blow off some steam with Alva, so she sat down to check her email right away. She only had one message addressed to <u>Tallgirl@city.com</u>, but it was not from Alva. It said:

Tallgirl@city.com

Tallu,

We must not meet before 9:00 A.M. Friday. We cannot afford to be seen together, just in case. Everything is on schedule. I will see you in the Metro Bank lobby as planned.

Barber

Lu did not know what to make of this note, especially since no one ever called her Tallu. It must have gone to the wrong email address, she thought as she printed a copy of the message. She was not sure what this message meant until it suddenly hit her that she was reading a note about a bank robbery! Someone named Barber was going to rob the Metro Bank!

Tallulah quickly signed off the Internet and tried to decide what to do next, realizing that the only sensible approach was to contact the police and tell them what she had received. She left a brief note for her mother on the kitchen table and hurried out the door.

Use with pages 90–91.

GO ON

Continued from page 88

The Springfield police station was not too far away, but the officer on duty was not exactly receptive when Lu got there. He smirked at her for a moment when she explained what had happened and handed him the note.

"Yeah, we'll look into it," he said gruffly, dismissing her as he turned to another case.

Tallulah walked home slowly, wondering if there was something else she should do, but finally she decided that this case was now in the hands of the police. She had done her duty, and if the police decided not to follow up, it would not be her fault.

The next morning, Lu was sitting in Social Studies class reading Chapter 3 in her textbook when a voice suddenly blared over the loudspeaker: "Tallulah Preston, please report to the principal's office immediately."

Oh no, she thought, *now what have I done?* She gathered up her books and headed for the door, trying hard to ignore the fact that everyone in the classroom was staring at her and whispering.

When she got to the office, two police officers were waiting for her. Lu tensed momentarily until she realized the two officers were smiling at her.

"Congratulations," said Officer Lopez as she shook Lu's hand.

"And thank you," said Officer Morse. "This morning you prevented a bank robbery! Thanks to you, we sent some plainclothes detectives to the bank this morning, just in case, and caught two thieves red-handed—a short young man named Barber and a tall girl named Tallu. You're a hero, and Mayor Barkley would like to have you come down to City Hall this afternoon for a press conference."

Lu gaped at the two police officers, then glanced over their shoulders at the principal to see if this was true.

Mrs. Jackson grinned at her and clapped her hands together.

"Well, this is so exciting," she gushed. "I'm going to make a schoolwide announcement right now!"

When Lu got back to her classroom, every student in the room stood and cheered as she came through the door. Lu could not stop smiling as she took a little bow and sat down in her seat, all the while thinking, "I can't wait to tell Alva about this!"

GO ON ➡

Use with pages 90–91.

Directions: Use "Tallgirl Saves the Day" to answer the following questions.

1. What is the setting at the beginning of this story?

(A) Metro Bank

(B) 24th Street School

(C) the police station

(D) Worcester High School

2. What did Lu do first on Thursday?

(A) She walked into homeroom late.

(B) She had a cup of tea for lunch.

(C) She stayed after school.

(D) She read Chapter 3 of her Social Studies textbook.

3. Where did Lu feel most comfortable on that Thursday?

(A) at school

(B) in the police station

(C) at the bank

(D) in her apartment

4. Why did Tallulah check her email when she got home?

(A) She was looking for a homework assignment.

(B) She had to write a Social Studies report.

(C) She wanted to report a crime.

(D) She was hoping to hear from Alva.

5. The story says, "School was a nightmare for Lu." This sentence means that _____.

(A) Lu had a nightmare at school

(B) Lu had a terrible day at school

(C) Lu fell asleep and had a dream

(D) Lu dreamed that she was in school

6. What happened just after Lu read her email?

(A) Two people robbed a bank.

(B) Her mother came home from work.

(C) Lu went to the police station.

(D) Lu got called to the principal's office.

Use with pages 88–89.

GO ON

Continued from page 90

7. **What kind of literature selection is this?**

- Ⓐ realistic fiction
- Ⓑ biography
- Ⓒ science fiction
- Ⓓ news article

8. **What did Tallulah most likely do after school on Friday?**

- Ⓐ She visited the robbers at the police station.
- Ⓑ She went to Mayor Barkley's office.
- Ⓒ She rented a video about bank robbers.
- Ⓓ She opened an account at the bank.

9. **Judging from the information in this story, who seemed most excited about what Tallulah did?**

- Ⓐ Alva
- Ⓑ Officer Lopez
- Ⓒ Mrs. Jackson
- Ⓓ Officer Morse

10. **How were the bank robbers caught?**

_____

_____

_____

_____

_____

Use with pages 88–89.

Directions: Read the story. Then answer questions 1 through 10.

The Legend of Flying Horse Lake
A Tale From China

A long time ago, the mountainous land called Ta-Li was surrounded by 19 high peaks. The mountains, lakes, and forests of Ta-Li were usually quite beautiful, but a terrible drought had taken hold of the land and no rain had fallen in three years. As the world turned to dust, the people sank into despair.

In one of the villages of Ta-Li, there lived a young man named Chun. His parents were old and frail at the time of the drought and could not survive such hardship. Young Chun was deeply saddened when both of his parents soon died.

When the other villagers visited him to pay their respects for his grievous loss, Chun decided that he would try to help those people who were left. Everyone had heard of a mountaintop lake that never ran dry, but no one knew where it was. Chun pledged to climb all 19 peaks until he found the lake, so he could somehow bring water to his village.

Chun set out at dawn the next day with a hoe, a bow and arrows, and a small supply of food and drink. He climbed for ten days straight to the top of the highest mountain, the Peak of Horses and Dragons. There he dug in the dirt for many hours but never found a trace of water. Exhausted, he lay down on the ground that night but was too worried to fall asleep. Then, suddenly, as he lay there looking up at the sky, he saw flashes of light land on a nearby mountain called Treasure Peak. Chun was so intrigued that he got up immediately and headed for the site where he had seen the flashes.

When he reached the top of Treasure Peak, Chun dug for hours but saw no sign of water anywhere. Exhausted again, he climbed a tree for safety and fell asleep.

Not much later, Chun was awakened by the arrival of several beautiful, white flying horses that landed near his tree. One horse tapped its hoof three times on a rock lying on the ground, and it swung open like a gate, revealing a sparkling, clear pool of water. The horses drank from the pool and soon departed.

Use with pages 94–95.

GO ON ➡

Continued from page 92

As soon as the sun rose, Chun climbed down from his tree and approached the rock. He tapped the stone three times with his hoe and the stone opened wide. Chun was so excited that he took only a quick swallow of water for himself and began digging a trench with his hoe so the water would flow down the mountainside to the people of his village.

Quite abruptly, an old white-haired man in a long, flowing robe appeared in a wisp of smoke and commanded Chun to stop digging.

"Young man," he said, "I am the guardian of this water, called Flying Horse Lake. It is the only water the flying horses drink, and you must not disturb it."

Chun paused in his labor and told the old man about the effects of the terrible drought on his village, about the death of his parents, and about all the other people who would soon die if he did not bring help.

The old man was moved by Chun's sad tale and agreed that the villagers could have all the water they needed. "However," he confided, "whoever takes the water will be turned to stone. As you are young and have your life before you, you should go back to your village and bid an old man to come and open the lake so the old man may become a stone and not yourself."

Chun appreciated the guardian's concern, but he could not postpone his task any longer. Too many people were depending on him, so he thanked the old man and began to dig. Before long he had finished a trench and released the water, which flowed quickly down the mountainside, turning everything in its path green and fresh.

When the water reached the village, the people rejoiced in their good fortune and somehow knew that it was Chun who had saved them.

Chun smiled as he looked down at the valley turning green before his eyes. He began to take a step toward the path leading home, but he could not move. When he looked down, he realized he no longer had any feet, his arms began to stiffen, and he soon turned completely into stone.

The villagers never saw Chun again, even when they hiked to the top of Treasure Peak to search for him. But they found his hoe lying on the ground next to a large upright stone beside the lake, and they knew at that moment that the stone was young Chun. To this day, the villagers visit the stone every year to bring flowers and heartfelt thanks for the young man who gave his life to save so many others.

GO ON ▶

Use with pages 94–95.

Directions: Use "The Legend of Flying Horse Lake" to answer the following questions.

1. Why did Chun decide to go in search of the mountaintop lake?

Ⓐ He wanted to save his parents.

Ⓑ His crops were dying from the drought.

Ⓒ He wanted to help the villagers.

Ⓓ The flying horses were dying.

2. The story says, "The world turned to dust." This means that _____.

Ⓐ houses fell apart

Ⓑ the village got dirty

Ⓒ people stopped sweeping

Ⓓ everything dried up

3. What happened just before Chun climbed to the Peak of Horses and Dragons?

Ⓐ Chun fell asleep in a tree.

Ⓑ His parents died.

Ⓒ He saw several flying horses.

Ⓓ An old man appeared.

4. What made the flashes of light that Chun saw that night?

Ⓐ a large stone

Ⓑ the guardian of the lake

Ⓒ sparks from the hoe

Ⓓ the flying horses

5. In the following sentence, what does the word *intrigued* mean?

"Chun was so intrigued that he got up immediately."

Ⓐ curious; very interested

Ⓑ thirsty or hungry

Ⓒ tired; completely exhausted

Ⓓ worried or suspicious

6. Which word best describes Chun?

Ⓐ dull-witted

Ⓑ honest

Ⓒ unselfish

Ⓓ vain

Use with pages 92–93.

GO ON ➡

Continued from page 94

7. What was needed to open up the rock on Treasure Peak?

Ⓐ three taps on the rock

Ⓑ flashes of light

Ⓒ three magic words

Ⓓ a wisp of smoke

8. Why did the old man decide to let Chun take the water?

Ⓐ He knew the flying horses would not return.

Ⓑ He was moved by Chun's story.

Ⓒ He wanted to teach Chun a lesson.

Ⓓ He was afraid that Chun would attack him.

9. How did the villagers figure out what had happened to Chun?

Ⓐ They heard his voice in the wind.

Ⓑ They spoke to the old white-haired man.

Ⓒ They found his hoe beside the stone.

Ⓓ They asked the flying horses.

10. Why do the people of Ta-Li visit the stone at Flying Horse Lake every year?

_____

_____

_____

_____

_____

Use with pages 92–93.

Directions: Read the passage. Decide whether each underlined section contains an error. Then look at the answer choices on page 97. Find the answer that corrects the error. If there is no error, choose "No Mistake."

Bigfoot Hoax Revealed

For decades, many people living in northern California and southern

Oregon <u>believing</u> in the existence of Bigfoot, an ape-like creature thought
      (1)

to be nine feet tall. Unfortunately, Bigfoot died on November 26, 2002,

at the <u>age of 84, his real name</u> was Ray L. Wallace.
        (2)

    Mr. Wallace invented Bigfoot in 1958. He had a friend carve some very

large wooden feet and used them to leave Bigfoot's tracks at logging sites in the

<u>California woods</u>. Wallace's son, Michael, <u>say that his dad</u> made the huge
    (3)   (4)

footprints as a prank, but then the story took on a life of its own. Some years

later, Mr. Wallace made a film of a person dressed in a large ape suit and

claimed <u>they was</u> a movie of Bigfoot tramping through the woods.
      (5)

    Some people refuse to believe that Bigfoot was a hoax, and some

claim they have seen Bigfoot on <u>many occassions</u>. Others have been
                               (6)

searching for him for many years and are not willing to give up the idea

that the creature is lurking out there somewhere.

Use with page 97.

GO ON ➡

Directions: Select the answer that corrects each error in "Bigfoot Hoax Revealed."
If there is no error, choose "No Mistake."

1. Ⓐ believe
   Ⓑ were believing
   Ⓒ have believed
   Ⓓ No Mistake

2. Ⓐ age of 84. His real name
   Ⓑ age of 84 his real name
   Ⓒ age of 84, His real name
   Ⓓ No Mistake

3. Ⓐ California Woods
   Ⓑ california Woods
   Ⓒ california woods
   Ⓓ No Mistake

4. Ⓐ saying that his dad
   Ⓑ say that his Dad
   Ⓒ says that his dad
   Ⓓ No Mistake

5. Ⓐ it was
   Ⓑ they were
   Ⓒ it were
   Ⓓ No Mistake

6. Ⓐ many ocassions
   Ⓑ many occasions
   Ⓒ many occazions
   Ⓓ No Mistake

STOP

Use with page 96.

Directions: Read the passage. Then answer questions 1 through 10.

Breaking Barriers

In recent years, professional women's tennis has been dominated by Venus and Serena Williams, and professional men's golf has been led by Tiger Woods. All three of these champions are of African-American descent and, not that long ago, all three would have been banned from professional sports because of their color. These famous athletes owe at least a small debt of gratitude to a remarkable woman named Althea Gibson for breaking racial barriers in professional sports. She was the first African American to play professional tennis or professional golf in the United States—and she played them both!

Althea Gibson was born in 1927 in Silver, South Carolina. Her parents, Daniel and Annie Gibson, were sharecroppers. They decided to move their family to New York City when Althea was three years old. Althea grew up in Harlem in the 1930s, during the Great Depression. A tall, rangy girl, Althea loved to play basketball and other sports with the boys in her neighborhood. During the summer of 1941, Althea won a paddleball tournament sponsored by the Police Athletic League. One of the supervisors who watched her play suggested that she try her hand at tennis, so she did.

In the 1940s, Althea Gibson began taking tennis lessons and winning tennis tournaments. From 1947 onward, she won ten straight national championships of the all-black American Tennis Association (ATA). But she was prohibited from playing in the all-white tennis events sponsored by the U.S. Lawn Tennis Association (USLTA).

For several years, many athletes and officials lobbied on behalf of Althea Gibson, including former Wimbledon and U.S. National champion Alice Marble. Finally, on August 28, 1950, Ms. Gibson was allowed to play in the U.S. National Championship at Forest Hills in New York. She was the first African-American female to compete in that or any other USLTA event. That year she won her first match against Barbara Knapp of England but lost to her next opponent in the second round.

Althea Gibson continued to dominate ATA tournaments for several years and began playing more USLTA competitions. In 1955, she traveled

Use with pages 100–101.

GO ON ➡

Continued from page 98

throughout Southeast Asia playing tennis on the Goodwill Tour sponsored by the U.S. government. When she returned for the 1956 season, she won 16 USLTA matches and the French Championship, defeating England's Angela Mortimer in the finals. With that victory, she became the first African American to win a major title in singles tennis.

In 1957, Gibson made sports history by winning the All-England Tennis Championship at Wimbledon. When she returned from England, New Yorkers welcomed her with a ticker-tape parade and the Medallion of the City. Soon afterward, she won the U.S. National Championship and became the top-ranked women's tennis player in the world. She also became the first African-American woman to win both of these championships and was chosen Female Athlete of the Year by the Associated Press. In the following years she won both tournaments again and then decided to retire from tennis.

Althea Gibson was a marvelous athlete and had become a celebrity at age 31, but she was just getting started. In 1958, she wrote her autobiography, *I Always Wanted to Be Somebody.* In 1959, she made a record album, *Althea Gibson Sings.* She also acted in a movie called *The Horse Soldiers.* In 1960, she traveled with the Harlem Globetrotters basketball team. Then she decided to take up professional golf. In 1964, she joined the Ladies Professional Golf Association (LPGA) and became the first African-American woman to play in an LPGA event. In the course of a seven-year career, she played in 171 golf tournaments, winning one of them.

In later years, Althea Gibson worked as a tennis teacher. She also served as the athletic commissioner for the state of New Jersey. She was inducted into the International Tennis Hall of Fame in 1971. In 1980, she entered the International Women's Sports Hall of Fame.

Perhaps more important than her many awards, however, was what Althea achieved as a pioneer in sports, as a woman, and as an African American. In the course of her remarkable career, she broke many barriers that had prevented others from competing in both amateur and professional sports. Her achievements helped to pave the way for many outstanding athletes, including Arthur Ashe, Zina Garrison, the Williams sisters, and Tiger Woods.

GO ON ➡

Use with pages 100–101.

Directions: Use "Breaking Barriers" to answer the following questions.

1. How did Althea Gibson break down racial barriers?

Ⓐ She played professional women's tennis.

Ⓑ She won a paddleball tournament.

Ⓒ She was the first African American to play professional tennis and professional golf in the U.S.

Ⓓ She was a marvelous athlete who tried lots of different sports.

2. Which would be another good title for this passage?

Ⓐ "The Road to Wimbledon"

Ⓑ "Tennis Superstars"

Ⓒ "Althea Gibson: African-American Athlete"

Ⓓ "Athlete of the Century"

3. The author's main purpose in this passage is to _____.

Ⓐ give information about Althea Gibson

Ⓑ compare Althea Gibson with Tiger Woods

Ⓒ tell an entertaining story about golf

Ⓓ persuade people to play tennis

4. Based on the passage, in what way are Althea Gibson and Serena Williams alike?

Ⓐ Both grew up in South Carolina.

Ⓑ Both dominated their sports in the 1950s.

Ⓒ Both have played both golf and tennis professionally.

Ⓓ Both are African-American tennis champions.

5. Which sentence states an opinion?

Ⓐ Althea Gibson was born in 1927 in Silver, South Carolina.

Ⓑ She is the greatest African-American athlete of all time.

Ⓒ Althea Gibson won her first Wimbledon title in 1957.

Ⓓ New Yorkers welcomed her with a ticker-tape parade.

Use with pages 98–99.

GO ON ➡

Continued from page 100

6. Before Althea Gibson won both Wimbledon and the U.S. National Championship in the same year, she _____.

Ⓐ joined the LPGA

Ⓑ was chosen Female Athlete of the Year

Ⓒ made a record album

Ⓓ traveled in Southeast Asia on the Goodwill Tour

7. Why wasn't Althea Gibson allowed to play in USLTA events before 1950?

Ⓐ She had not won any championships yet.

Ⓑ Former champion Alice Marble spoke on her behalf.

Ⓒ Only white players were allowed in those events.

Ⓓ She was not a very good player.

8. For Althea Gibson, what was probably the most important thing she achieved?

Ⓐ winning the first all-black ATA Championship

Ⓑ breaking barriers for African-American athletes

Ⓒ expanding her career to singing and acting

Ⓓ traveling on tour with the Harlem Globetrotters

9. This passage would most likely be found in a _____.

Ⓐ news magazine

Ⓑ sports biography

Ⓒ literary anthology

Ⓓ short story collection

10. In addition to championship trophies she won, what other important honors and awards did Althea Gibson receive? Give a brief summary.

_____

_____

_____

_____

_____

_____

_____

Use with pages 98–99.

Directions: Read the passage. Then answer questions 1 through 10.

The Furious Storm

by Larry O'Hanlon

Here's a tip from the experts: If you're in New Orleans when the "Big One" hits, have a lifeboat handy. Some scientists warn that the right *hurricane*–a tropical cyclone with at least 74-mile-per-hour winds–could strike the Gulf Coast in a way that would hurl millions of gallons of water to turn the city known as the "Big Easy" into the "Big Soup Bowl."

A major flood could submerge much of central New Orleans beneath 20 feet of water, leaving many of the metropolitan area's 1.3 million residents clinging to rooftops–a prospect that has engineers and city planners scrambling for defensive strategies. "It's the luck of the draw," says hurricane expert Hugh Willoughby at the National Oceanic and Atmospheric Administration (NOAA). He thinks it's a matter of when– not if–the "Big One" will pound New Orleans during the annual hurricane season between June and November.

Why is New Orleans so vulnerable? There are three main reasons:

1. Sandwiched between Lake Pontchartrain and the Mississippi River, most of the city lies below sea level. A flood that gushes over shielding *levees* (earthen walls built over the years since the 1700s to protect against river overflow) would submerge New Orleans in water.

2. *Marshes,* freshwater and saltwater swamps of mud and diverse plant life, divide New Orleans from the Gulf of Mexico. They once acted as barriers from *storm surges*–high water accompanying storms. Now the marshes are quickly *eroding,* or wearing away. This is partly because levees block and reroute the Mississippi's periodic flooding cycles, which spread mud and *sediment* (rock particles) that shore up marshes. In some places, the Gulf shoreline has receded 32 to 48 kilometers (20 to 30 miles) closer to New Orleans.

3. The number and intensity of Atlantic Ocean hurricanes tend to increase in cycles every few decades, experts say. "We've just entered a more active phase," says Willoughby.

Use with pages 105–107.

GO ON ▶

Continued from page 102

New Orleans hasn't always faced such danger. When first built in 1718, the city sat on higher land beside the Mississippi. But it was erected on soft river mud—a mix of *silt* (loose rock particles) and clay minerals—deposited over millions of years by flowing water at the *delta,* or mouth, where the Mississippi meets the Gulf. The trouble is, the soft ground beneath central New Orleans has sunk nine feet in nearly 300 years. (Most New Orleans skyscrapers are supported by deep piles, so they don't rely on the soft ground for support.)

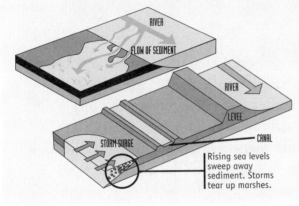

Coastal Defenses: Going, Going, Gone?

Marshes south and east of New Orleans once shielded the city from storms. But they're eroding quickly.

Then: Natural Flow
The Mississippi's periodic floods once spread sediment and mud—building up protective marshes.

Now: Vanishing Marshes
Levees (earthen walls) and canals reroute the river. Sediment washes away in the sea.

Perfect Storm

Not just any hurricane could engulf New Orleans, Willoughby explains; otherwise, the city would have drowned long ago. New Orleans' nightmare will be a "perfect" storm—one that strikes in *just* the right way.

Every year, an average of five or six hurricanes that form in the Atlantic Ocean churn toward Central and North America—often with Florida and the Caribbean Islands dead in their paths. But changes in wind direction and the earth's air currents cause most hurricanes to sweep around and roll up the U.S. East Coast, weakening as they move over colder seawater. About once a year, however, a hurricane stomps right over Florida, where warm water in the Gulf of Mexico can reenergize it as a monster storm, thrusting it westward.

Use with pages 105–107.

Continued from page 103

The perfect storm could either strike New Orleans east of the city, with gale-force winds blowing south, shoveling water from Lake Pontchartrain over the lake levees; or the storm could strike west of the city, causing winds to heave Gulf of Mexico seawater up the Mississippi River and crash over its levees.

Joseph Suhayda, former director of the Louisiana Water Resources Research Institute at Louisiana State University, uses computer models to study potential hurricane hits. His surprising finding: A severe but not catastrophic Category 3 storm would be enough to swamp New Orleans if it slowed down and hovered east of the city. "A slow storm has more time to build up the wind effect over the lake," says Suhayda. "Waves can add four to five feet to surging lake waters," he adds.

River Walls

Engineers and city planners are racing to soften a hurricane's potential blow to New Orleans. In addition to hashing out elaborate evacuation plans, one strategy calls for slowing the loss of marshlands by building control gates. These would let the Mississippi overflow once again, spreading sediment-rich water to rebuild marshes. Another idea: shoring up barrier islands in the gulf. But no plan would remove the hurricane threat immediately, and public officials say that the costs for all of these schemes are prohibitive.

With early storm detection, most of New Orleans can be safely evacuated, Suhayda says. For those who can't get out, Suhayda offers his own controversial scheme: Engineers would construct a 20-foot-high east/west wall along the north edge of the French Quarter, which would seal off a downtown section. The existing Mississippi River levees would surround the "haven" on three sides and are high enough now for Category 5 hurricane protection. The sealed-off "bowl" could provide safety for several hundred thousand people.

But even with a walled-off safe haven, it could take months to pump the rest of New Orleans dry. What's more, water damage and toxic chemical leaks from flooded industrial facilities in the area would probably make much of New Orleans impossible to live in, says Willoughby: "We may need a new New Orleans."

Use with pages 105–107.

GO ON

Directions: Use "The Furious Storm" to answer the following questions.

1. **What is the main idea of this article?**

   Ⓐ The city of New Orleans has long been known as the "Big Easy."

   Ⓑ Hurricane season lasts from June to November.

   Ⓒ A strong hurricane could easily flood most of New Orleans.

   Ⓓ The Mississippi River flows through the city of New Orleans.

2. **Why is New Orleans so vulnerable to flooding from a storm?**

   Ⓐ It is located in Louisiana.

   Ⓑ The city lies north of the Gulf of Mexico.

   Ⓒ Hurricanes often move through the Gulf of Mexico.

   Ⓓ Most of the city lies below sea level.

3. **How has most of New Orleans changed since it was first built in 1718?**

   Ⓐ It has sunk nine feet into the ground.

   Ⓑ Most houses and buildings are now made of stone.

   Ⓒ The population of the city has decreased.

   Ⓓ Most structures have been moved away from the river.

4. **In general, most hurricanes that form in the Atlantic Ocean hit what part of the United States?**

   Ⓐ Midwest

   Ⓑ East Coast

   Ⓒ Southwest

   Ⓓ Gulf Coast

GO ON ▷

Use with pages 102–104.

Continued from page 105

5. Most of the information in this article is organized in terms of _____.

   Ⓐ comparison and contrast

   Ⓑ questions and answers

   Ⓒ chronological order

   Ⓓ problems and solutions

6. In the following sentence, what does the word *controversial* mean?

"For those who can't get out, Suhayda offers his own controversial scheme."

   Ⓐ causing argument or dispute

   Ⓑ very expensive

   Ⓒ proven by scientific experiment

   Ⓓ foolish; not practical

7. The article says that in some places the Gulf shoreline has receded 20 to 30 miles closer to New Orleans. From this fact, you can conclude that the city _____.

   Ⓐ is less likely to be flooded

   Ⓑ will eventually stop sinking

   Ⓒ is more likely to be flooded

   Ⓓ no longer needs a marsh barrier

8. Look at the diagrams of coastal defenses. How do levees make floods more likely?

   Ⓐ They cause the river to overflow in periodic floods.

   Ⓑ They prevent sediment from building up in protective marshes.

   Ⓒ They reroute the river, causing increased flow.

   Ⓓ They funnel sediment into canals, causing them to overflow.

Use with pages 102–104.

GO ON ▶

Continued from page 106

9. The author's main purpose in this article is to _____.

Ⓐ entertain readers with a story about people in New Orleans

Ⓑ give information about potential dangers in New Orleans

Ⓒ persuade people to move out of New Orleans

Ⓓ compare New Orleans with other major cities

10. What plans have engineers come up with to help protect New Orleans from the effects of a hurricane? Write a brief summary of the plans.

_____

_____

_____

_____

_____

Use with pages 102–104.

Directions: Read this poem. Then answer questions 1 through 6.

Southbound on the Freeway

by May Swenson

A tourist came in from Orbitville,
parked in the air, and said:

The creatures of this star
are made of metal and glass.

Through the transparent parts   5
you can see their guts.

Their feet are round and roll
on diagrams or long

measuring tapes, dark
with white lines.   10

They have four eyes.
The two in the back are red.

Sometimes you can see a five-eyed
one, with a red eye turning

on top of his head.   15
He must be special—

the others respect him
and go slow

when he passes, winding
among them from behind.   20

They all hiss as they glide,
like inches, down the marked

tapes. Those soft shapes,
shadowy inside

the hard bodies—are they   25
their guts or their brains?

Use with page 109.

GO ON ➡

Name _____

Directions: Use "Southbound on the Freeway" to answer the following questions.

1. The "tourist" in this poem (line 1) came from _____.

   Ⓐ somewhere in Europe

   Ⓑ outer space

   Ⓒ an American city

   Ⓓ the ocean

2. Where does this "tourist" park to observe?

   Ⓐ in an underground garage

   Ⓑ on the ocean near the shore

   Ⓒ at a roadside cafe

   Ⓓ in the air over the freeway

3. What are the "creatures" (line 3) seen by the "tourist"?

   Ⓐ cars

   Ⓑ airplanes

   Ⓒ horses

   Ⓓ people

4. In lines 8–10, what are the "diagrams or long/measuring tapes, dark/with white lines"?

   Ⓐ maps

   Ⓑ highways

   Ⓒ books

   Ⓓ skyscrapers

5. By the end of the poem, the "tourist" seems to feel _____.

   Ⓐ disappointed

   Ⓑ upset

   Ⓒ puzzled

   Ⓓ excited

6. What does the "tourist" conclude from his or her observations of the freeway?

   _____

   _____

   _____

   _____

Use with page 108.

Directions: Read the passage. Then answer questions 1 through 10.

"Remember Wounded Knee"

by Sean McCollum

American Indians have twice battled the U.S. government near a little creek in South Dakota.

By late December 1890, the American Indian tribes of the Sioux Nation were bracing for trouble. About 120 men and 230 women and children of Chief Big Foot's Miniconjou (min-nih-KAHN-joo) band were running from a growing number of U.S. cavalry in South Dakota. The soldiers had been sent to quell a rumored uprising—and put a stop to the new Ghost Dance religion.

The Miniconjou hoped to find protection with other Sioux at the Pine Ridge Reservation. But on December 28, the 7th Cavalry intercepted them and ordered them to "move down to camp at Wounded Knee."

Wounded Knee—at this little creek near the southwestern edge of South Dakota, the U.S. military campaign to eliminate Indian resistance came to a bloody conclusion. What occurred there burdened its name with all the misunderstanding and conflict that has plagued relations between Indians and the American government. But years later, Wounded Knee would become a rallying call for Indian rebirth.

Well before the incident at Wounded Knee, the seven tribes that make up the Sioux Nation had already been shattered. Despite promises by U.S. leaders and guarantees made in an 1868 treaty, the large Sioux territory had been whittled to small reservations on hardscrabble land. Clashes with troops, demands to adopt white ways, and eradication of their bison herds had left many in despair.

Dance of Desperation

In the late 1880s, a new religion had brought hope. Wovoka, a Paiute Indian, had dreamed that Jesus Christ—returning as an Indian—had promised that if the people were good and peaceful, and danced the Ghost Dance, then the Great Spirit would "bring back all game of every kind."

GO ON ➡

Continued from page 110

"All dead Indians come back and live again," Wovoka's dream went on. "Big flood comes like water and all white people die . . . After that, nobody but Indians everywhere . . ."

The Ghost Dance religion spread like prairie fire among the Plains nations. "They snatched at the hope," said Red Cloud, a Sioux chief. "The white men were frightened and called for soldiers."

At Wounded Knee on December 29, 1890, Colonel James W. Forsyth ordered Big Foot's people to surrender their guns. The Miniconjou hated giving up their means for hunting and defense, and feared revenge at the hands of the 7th Cavalry. Fourteen years earlier, the 7th's commanding officer, George Custer, and all 210 of his men had been killed after attacking a large Sioux encampment, in the Battle of the Little Bighorn–known as Custer's Last Stand. Now, soldiers from the 7th seemed itchy for payback.

Under the Guns

Forsyth stationed his troops around the Miniconjou camp. Some of the tribe brought out their rifles and stacked them, but Forsyth was not satisfied. He sent his men to search the warriors and the tepees. The Miniconjou men tensed. A medicine man danced a few steps of the Ghost Dance. Soldiers readied their weapons.

Accounts vary on what happened next, but most agree that, deliberately or not, a shot was fired. The soldiers' guns crashed in response. The warriors grabbed for their guns and fought back. Within minutes, the hottest fighting was over, and most of the Indian men lay dead or dying. The soldiers then hunted down and killed many of the fleeing survivors, mostly women and children.

"We tried to run," Louise Weasel Bear said later, "but they shot us like we were buffalo."

Of 350 people in Big Foot's group, between 180 and 300 were killed; of about 500 soldiers, 31 died, most from their own crossfire. The Wounded Knee massacre was the final battle of the Indian Wars, which had lasted 350 years, since the arrival of white settlers. Nicholas Black Elk recalled in his memoir, *Black Elk Speaks:*

GO ON

Use with pages 114–115.

Continued from page 111

I can still see the butchered women and children lying . . .
along the crooked gulch as plain as when I saw them with
eyes still young. A people's dream died there. It was a
beautiful dream.

The 1973 Siege

Decades later, Wounded Knee once again became the focal point of
Indian resistance. In late February 1973, more than 200 Native American
activists and militants, some of them armed with hunting rifles and
shotguns, took over a tiny village near the massacre site. They were joined
by members of the American Indian Movement (AIM), an activist
organization that fought for civil rights for Native Americans. AIM took as
its rallying call: "Remember Wounded Knee." Protester Madonna Gilbert
recalled in the book *In the Spirit of Crazy Horse*:

> The [Lakota] elders said, What can we do to wake these
> Indians up? We have to take a stand somewhere! So we
> decided that the symbolic place would be Wounded Knee.

The takeover began as a protest against corruption in the Pine Ridge
tribal council. But the focus immediately swelled to broader historical
issues. As *The New York Times* reported:

> The embattled Indians relayed demands . . . that the Senate . . .
> hold hearings on treaties made with Indians, that the Senate
> start a "full-scale investigation" of government treatment of
> the Indians.

The government, beleaguered by nationwide civil rights and Vietnam
War demonstrations, responded with a show of force. U.S. marshals and
FBI agents, armed with military-grade weaponry including armored
personnel carriers, surrounded the tiny hamlet. The two sides engaged in
sporadic gunfights, killing two protesters and paralyzing a federal marshal.

Many feared (and some hoped) that the government would launch
a full-scale attack against the men, women, and children who occupied
Wounded Knee. But national and international opinion helped
prevent such a move. After 71 days, the two sides negotiated an end
to the standoff.

GO ON ➡

Use with pages 114–115.

Continued from page 112

Thirty years later, Indian distrust and resentment of the U.S. government continues to run deep. Yet at the same time, the 1973 events ushered in a resurgence of Indian pride, and greater respect for Indian culture and sovereignty. Indians have since fought and won numerous land-rights cases in the courts, and gained greater public awareness of the challenges their people face.

And what of Wounded Knee? The Pine Ridge Reservation, where Wounded Knee is located, remains the poorest area in the U.S.; unemployment is 86 percent. In a nation where average life expectancy is 74 for men and 79 for women, Pine Ridge men live on average to only 48, and women, to 52.

GO ON

Use with pages 114–115.

Directions: Use "Remember Wounded Knee" to answer the following questions.

1. In the following sentence, what does the word *quell* mean?

   "The soldiers had been sent to quell a rumored uprising."

   Ⓐ a terrible battle

   Ⓑ to put down; stop

   Ⓒ a small bird

   Ⓓ to arrange in order

2. What would be another good title for this passage?

   Ⓐ "Native American Reservations"

   Ⓑ "The Beginnings of the Ghost Dance"

   Ⓒ "The Sioux Nation of Seven Tribes"

   Ⓓ "Rebellions at Wounded Knee"

3. In late 1890, people of the Miniconjou band began moving toward the Pine Ridge Reservation because they _____.

   Ⓐ were fleeing the growing number of U.S. cavalry

   Ⓑ wanted to hold a Ghost Dance

   Ⓒ remembered what had happened at Wounded Knee

   Ⓓ signed a treaty with Chief Big Foot

4. What happened soon after the Miniconjou gave up their guns to Colonel Forsyth?

   Ⓐ The tribe moved to a camp at Wounded Knee.

   Ⓑ The soldiers shot many of the Indians.

   Ⓒ General Custer and his men died at Little Bighorn.

   Ⓓ Nicholas Black Elk had a beautiful dream.

5. In the 1880s, why was Wovoka's dream so appealing to so many Indians?

   Ⓐ It illustrated the need to accept Christianity.

   Ⓑ It provided all the information needed to create a fair treaty between the Indians and the U.S. government.

   Ⓒ It predicted that Indians and white people would live together in peace.

   Ⓓ It suggested that everything would go back to the way it was before white people arrived.

Use with pages 110–113.

GO ON ➡

Continued from page 114

6. **Which sentence states an opinion?**

Ⓐ The Sioux Nation was made up of seven tribal groups.

Ⓑ Red Cloud was a Sioux chief in the late 1800s.

Ⓒ The Lakota were the best warriors among the Sioux.

Ⓓ Big Foot's people camped at Wounded Knee in December 1890.

7. **The main goal of the protest at Wounded Knee in 1973 was to _____.**

Ⓐ gain better treatment from the U.S. government

Ⓑ build a memorial for victims of the massacre of 1890

Ⓒ force white Americans to leave South Dakota forever

Ⓓ improve the schools and job opportunities on the Pine Ridge Reservation

8. **This passage is an example of what genre?**

Ⓐ biography

Ⓑ realistic fiction

Ⓒ historical nonfiction

Ⓓ folktale

9. **How was the 1973 protest different from the incident in 1890?**

Ⓐ The U.S. government responded to it with force.

Ⓑ People on both sides were shot.

Ⓒ It took place in a village near Wounded Knee.

Ⓓ It was ended by negotiation.

10. **What are some of the gains from the 1973 protest at Wounded Knee?**

_____

_____

_____

_____

_____

_____

_____

Use with pages 110–113.

Narrative Writing Test 1

Directions: Read the following prompt. Then use the remaining space on the page to plan your essay. Write your essay on a separate sheet of paper.

Prompt

Have you had a first impression about someone that turned out to be wrong?

Before you write, think of a person whom you misjudged at first. What was your first impression? What did that person do or say to make you change your mind?

Write an essay telling what happened to make you see the person in a new way.

Planning Area

Name _____

Narrative Writing Test 2

Directions: Read the following prompt. Then use the remaining space on the page to plan your essay. Write your essay on a separate sheet of paper.

Prompt

Suppose that one day you walk down an unfamiliar trail in the park. Suddenly, you find yourself in a strange place. Plants and animals talk to people, and unusual things seem to happen. What kind of adventure do you think you might have?

Before you write, think about what might happen in the place described. What might the plants and animals say? How might you react? What might happen next?

Tell a story about your adventure on the trail.

Planning Area

Narrative Writing Test 3

Directions: Read the following prompt. Then use the remaining space on the page to plan your essay. Write your essay on a separate sheet of paper.

Prompt

Have you ever waited for something special to arrive in the mail?

Before you write, think about the item you were waiting for. What was it? Why were you looking forward to its arrival? What happened after it arrived?

Write an essay telling of the time you waited for something in the mail.

Planning Area

Expository Writing Test 1

Directions: Read the following prompt. Then use the remaining space on the page to plan your essay. Write your essay on a separate sheet of paper.

Prompt

You get home after school and you're starving! No one else is home and nothing has been prepared. If you want dinner, you'll have to make it yourself.

Before you write, think about the ingredients you will use. Will you cook or make a sandwich? Plan what steps you would take to prepare something you would like to eat.

Write an essay explaining step-by-step how you prepared your evening meal.

Planning Area

Expository Writing Test 2

Directions: Read the following prompt. Then use the remaining space on the page to plan your essay. Write your essay on a separate sheet of paper.

Prompt

Suppose you and your family had to leave your home because of a flood. You can take only three items with you. Tell what items you would take.

Before you write, think about all the things you have and which ones have a special meaning for you. Is there something practical you might want? Is there something special?

Write an essay telling what items you would take and explaining why you chose them.

Planning Area

Name _____

Expository Writing Test 3

Directions: Read the following prompt. Then use the remaining space on the page to plan your essay. Write your essay on a separate sheet of paper.

Prompt

Some people look forward to relaxing during vacations. Others plan special activities. How do you like to spend your vacations?

Before you write, think about what you usually do over vacation. Do you take a trip? Do you visit relatives? See a movie? Have fun with friends?

Write an essay explaining how you spend your time during vacations.

Planning Area

Persuasive Writing Test 1

Directions: Read the following prompt. Then use the remaining space on the page to plan your essay. Write your essay on a separate sheet of paper.

Prompt

A movie or play you have seen has affected you very strongly. You think your classmates should see it, too.

Before you write, think about that movie or play. Why did it affect you so strongly? Why do you think others should see it?

Write an essay to convince your classmates to see the movie or play you saw.

Planning Area

Name _____

Persuasive Writing Test 2

Directions: Read the following prompt. Then use the remaining space on the page to plan your essay. Write your essay on a separate sheet of paper.

Prompt

Suppose that your town wants to build a statue honoring someone from history. Anyone in town can suggest the person to be honored. Who do you think it should be?

Before you write, think about the person you chose. What important thing did that person do or say? Why does he or she deserve to be honored?

Write an essay to convince people in your town that your choice is the best one.

Planning Area

Persuasive Writing Test 3

Directions: Read the following prompt. Then use the remaining space on the page to plan your essay. Write your essay on a separate sheet of paper.

Prompt

The governor of your state is searching for a student to help promote awareness of an environmental issue.

Before you write, think about problems that exist with the environment. Choose one to focus on. What is the problem? Why is it important to fix?

Write an essay to persuade your governor to select the environmental issue you support and to choose you to help promote it.

Planning Area

Name _____

Narrative Prompts

Directions: Use the following prompts for additional student practice with writing narrative stories and essays. See page 137 for an answer sheet. See pages 132–135 for examples of scoring rubrics.

Narrative Prompt 1

Have you ever done something surprising–something you never imagined you would or could do? Did you win something? Did you finally do something after months of practice?

Before you write, think about the surprising thing you did. What did you do? How did it make you feel?

Write an essay telling about the time you did something surprising.

Narrative Prompt 2

Imagine you could meet a famous person from history. Whom would you choose to meet?

Think about the person you chose. What would you say to him or her? What would he or she look like? What could you learn about people and events long ago?

Write a story about meeting a famous historical person.

Narrative Prompt 3

All friends have had misunderstandings at times.

Think about a misunderstanding you have had with a friend. What was it about? What led up to it? How did you resolve the misunderstanding?

Write an essay telling about a misunderstanding you have had with a friend.

Narrative Prompt 4

Imagine walking into an abandoned old house. Inside, you see a locked door leading to a mysterious room. You hear strange scratching sounds. What is going on?

Before you write, think about the mystery. Who or what is in the room? Why is the door locked? How do you open it? What happens when you do?

Write a story about the mysterious house.

Narrative Prompts

Directions: Use the following prompts for additional student practice
with writing narrative stories and essays. See page 137 for an answer sheet.
See pages 132–135 for examples of scoring rubrics.

Narrative Prompt 5

If you could go back to any time in
history, when would it be?

Before you write, think about what you
know about the period. What would
you do?

Write a story about a day you travel back
in time.

Narrative Prompt 6

Some memories stay with you for a
lifetime. Good times you have spent
with family and friends are the greatest
memories.

Think about a good time you had with
your family or friends. What did you do?
How did you have fun?

Write an essay telling about a good
experience you had with your family
or friends.

Narrative Prompt 7

Everybody has a day they would like to
forget. What is yours?

Before you write, think about what
happened that day. Was it embarrassing?
Sad? Scary?

Write an essay telling about the day you
would like to forget.

Narrative Prompt 8

Everyone is afraid of severe weather
conditions such as thunderstorms,
blizzards, or hurricanes. What kind of
weather frightens you?

Think about what this type of weather
feels like. How does it sound? Have you
ever experienced this kind of weather?
What happened? What did you or your
family members do to cope?

Write an essay telling about a day you
experienced this frightening weather.

Name _____

Expository Prompts

Directions: Use the following prompts for additional student practice with writing expository essays. See page 137 for an answer sheet. See pages 132–135 for examples of scoring rubrics.

Expository Prompt 1

What game or sport do you like to play? Imagine you are teaching a friend how to play it for the first time.

Think about what you need to know in order to play the game or sport. Who goes first? What happens next? How are points scored? How do you win?

Write an essay explaining how to play the game or sport.

Expository Prompt 2

Suppose you are writing a book about your area. What would a person from another country need to know in order to shop, use the parks, or order in a restaurant?

Before you write, think about your city or town. What would someone need to know to make the most of his or her visit? What are the sights to see? What are the good restaurants?

Write an essay explaining how to make the most out of a visit to your city or town.

Expository Prompt 3

You have just been told that you have to give up all modern conveniences, such as your microwave or television, except one. What convenience couldn't you live without?

Before you write, think about all the appliances in your home. Choose the one that you couldn't live without. What makes it useful to you? Why is it so important?

Write an essay explaining why you would keep this item.

Expository Prompt 4

Imagine you need to write the directions for using a common object such as a stapler, toaster, pair of scissors, or hammer.

Think about which object you want to write about. What are the steps someone needs to follow? How does it work? What is it used for?

Write an essay explaining how to use the object.

Expository Prompts

Directions: Use the following prompts for additional student practice with writing expository essays. See page 137 for an answer sheet. See pages 132–135 for examples of scoring rubrics.

Expository Prompt 5

Suppose this year's orange crop was very poor. As a result, people are complaining about the high price of orange juice at the supermarket. The local newspaper wants you to write an article about the situation.

Think about what might have caused the crop to fail. How does a shortage of oranges affect consumers? If people buy less juice, how does this affect the farmers? What can shoppers expect in the future?

Write an essay explaining the situation.

Expository Prompt 6

"Most Likely to Succeed," "Best Dressed," "Class Brain," "Friendliest"–which of these would you want as the caption under your high school yearbook picture?

Think about which caption best suits you. How does your personality fit the description you chose? Why do you want to be remembered this way?

Write an essay explaining why the caption you selected describes you.

Expository Prompt 7

There are many forms of exercise, from yoga to ice hockey, water ballet to rock climbing. Each affects the body differently.

Before you write, choose one form of exercise. Think about how the exercise benefits the body. What parts of the body does it strengthen? What equipment is needed? How does someone do this exercise?

Write an essay that explains why the exercise is important and give a brief explanation of how to do the exercise.

Expository Prompt 8

There are animals that would make good pets and others that should be kept in the wild.

Think about animals that should be kept in the wild. Choose one animal to write about. How does this animal eat? What is its habitat?

Write an essay explaining why this animal should be left in the wild.

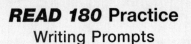

Persuasive Prompts

Directions: Use the following prompts for additional student practice with writing persuasive essays. See page 137 for an answer sheet. See pages 132–135 for examples of scoring rubrics.

Persuasive Prompt 1

Your club has come up with three ways to raise money: you could have a car wash, hold a chicken barbecue, or sell home-baked goods at a booth in the mall.

Before you write, think about which fund-raising activity you want the club to do. Will it raise the most money? Does it use the talents of your club members best?

Write an essay to persuade your club members that your choice is the best one.

Persuasive Prompt 2

Your local Chamber of Commerce has asked students to write essays encouraging people to move to your town or city.

Think of why people from other areas might like living in your town. Are there a lot of opportunities for good jobs? Does your area have nice weather?

Write an essay to persuade people to move to your town or city.

Persuasive Prompt 3

Your school is going to ask someone famous to speak to the student body. The principal asks students for suggestions for whom he or she should bring.

Before you write, think about famous people admired by students your age. Choose one. Why would this person be a good choice?

Write an essay to your principal to convince him or her to bring the person of your choice to speak to the student body.

Persuasive Prompt 4

Your guidance counselor has asked students to suggest speakers for Career Day. What career would you want to hear about, and why?

Before you write, think about why the career you chose would interest students. Perhaps the career offers many job opportunities or the chance to be creative, or it benefits people who need help.

Write an essay to persuade your guidance counselor to invite someone to speak about the career in which you are most interested.

Persuasive Prompts

Directions: Use the following prompts for additional student practice with writing persuasive essays. See page 137 for an answer sheet. See pages 132–135 for examples of scoring rubrics.

Persuasive Prompt 5

Your town has set aside an area for community recreation. The mayor has asked for ideas for its use.

Before you write, think about what you think the area should be. A skateboard park, an area to walk your dog, an outdoor theater, or something else?

How will the community benefit from your choice?

Write an essay to convince the mayor that your idea for the recreation area is best.

Persuasive Prompt 6

Your principal is thinking about changing the school's colors. In the announcements, the principal asked for suggestions for the new colors.

Before you write, think of colors you would like to represent your school. Make a decision. Why would these colors be good for the school? What do they represent?

Write an essay to convince the principal to choose your suggestion for the new school colors.

Persuasive Prompt 7

Your local Chamber of Commerce is going to choose a special place from your city or town to feature on their brochure. They have asked students to send in ideas. The only requirement is the place needs to be famous or unique to your town.

Before you write, think about the places that meet the criteria. Choose one. Is it a restaurant with a famous menu? Is it an odd-looking building? Is it a famous historical site?

Write an essay to convince the Chamber of Commerce to feature your idea.

Persuasive Prompt 8

Recent letters to the editor of your local newspaper have emphasized the bad habits of teenagers. The paper has asked students to write an essay in response to these comments.

Before you write, think about the good habits of teenagers. How do teenagers help a community? Why are teenagers misunderstood?

Write an essay to the newspaper to convince readers that teenagers do have good habits as well.

Additional Support

Use these rubrics, management forms, and other resources to organize and support instruction.

6-Point Rubric 132
4-Point Rubric 134
Reading Test Form 136
Writing Test Form 137
Idea Web 138
Outline 139
Student Writing Self-Assessment 140

Test Tips 141
Brain Boosters 142
Lesson Tracking 143
Test Tracking 144
Family Letter in English 145
Family Letter in Spanish 146
Answer Key 147

6-Point Rubric

Writing assessors may use this 6-point rubric as a scoring guide. Scores range from a low of 1 to a high of 6. Occasionally, a paper that is illegible or totally unrelated to the topic is graded U for unscorable.

6 Points

The writer demonstrates outstanding proficiency in addressing the specified writing task. The topic or main idea of the writing is extremely focused and well developed. Main points are elaborated with many well-chosen supporting details, examples, reasons, or explanations. The writing shows a carefully reasoned pattern of organization and demonstrates excellent control over the integration and flow of ideas. The writer demonstrates a fluent and mature command of language, including the choice of vivid and precise words, transitional phrases, and the use of engaging literary devices. The writing is complete, unified, and does not stray from its purpose. Sentences are complete, varied, and demonstrate correct grammatical conventions, such as accurate subject-verb agreement and pronoun usage. The rules of capitalization and punctuation are followed, and words are spelled correctly in all cases.

5 Points

The writer demonstrates strong proficiency in addressing the specified writing task. The topic or main idea of the writing is focused and well developed. Main points are elaborated with ample supporting details, examples, reasons, or explanations. The writing shows a coherent pattern of organization and demonstrates strong control of the integration and flow of ideas. The writer demonstrates a good command of language, including the choice of vivid and precise words, and transitional phrases. The writing is complete, unified, and does not stray from its purpose. Sentences are complete, varied, and are generally grammatically correct. The rules of capitalization and punctuation are followed, and words are spelled correctly in most cases.

4 Points

The writer demonstrates adequate proficiency in addressing the specified writing task. The topic or main idea of the writing is developed with some supporting details, examples, reasons, or explanations. The writing shows adequate organization and demonstrates control of the integration and flow of ideas. The writer demonstrates adequate command of language, including facility in the choice of words and use of transitional phrases. The writing is generally complete and unified but may occasionally stray from its purpose. Sentences are generally complete and varied but may display some errors in subject-verb agreement, pronoun usage, and other grammatical conventions. The rules of capitalization, punctuation, and spelling are followed in most cases.

3 Points

The writer demonstrates limited proficiency in addressing the specified writing task. The topic or main idea of the writing is developed with a limited number of supporting details, examples, reasons, or explanations, and some key ideas may be lacking. The writing shows a pattern of organization, but the writer occasionally strays from it or confuses the order of ideas. The writer demonstrates inadequate facility with language, including inappropriate word choice and a lack of transitional phrases. The writing lacks completeness, often straying from its purpose. Sentences, though generally complete, lack variety and display basic errors in grammar. There are also errors in capitalization, punctuation, and spelling.

2 Points

The writer demonstrates a low level of proficiency in addressing the specified writing task. The topic or main idea of the writing is poorly developed with few, if any, supporting details, examples, reasons, or explanations. There is some attempt at an overall plan, but the writer frequently strays from it or confuses the order of ideas. The writer demonstrates little facility with language. The writing lacks completeness and coherence. Sentences lack variety and display serious errors in structure and grammar. There are many errors in capitalization, punctuation, and spelling.

1 Point

The writer demonstrates fundamental deficiencies in addressing the specified writing task. The topic or main idea of the writing may be poorly developed or not explicitly stated. The writing shows little or no evidence of an organizational plan or strategy. The writer demonstrates deficient language skills and severely limited word choice. The writing lacks any sense of completeness. Sentences display serious and persistent errors in structure and mechanics that hinder the effectiveness of communication. There are frequent errors in capitalization, punctuation, and spelling.

Unscorable

The response is unrelated to the prompt, is simply a rewording of the prompt, or is plagiarized; OR the student refused to write, wrote illegibly, or wrote incomprehensibly; OR the response is related to the prompt, but does not carry enough information.

4-Point Rubric

Writing assessors may use this 4-point rubric as a scoring guide. Scores range from a low of 1 to a high of 4. Occasionally, a paper that is illegible or totally unrelated to the topic is graded U for unscorable.

4 Points

The writer clearly addresses the task specified in the writing prompt. The topic or main idea of the writing is focused and well developed. Main points are elaborated with ample supporting details, examples, reasons, or explanations. The writing shows a clear pattern of organization and demonstrates control over the integration and flow of ideas. The writer demonstrates a mature command of language, including the choice of vivid and precise words, transitional phrases, and the use of engaging literary devices. The writing is complete, unified, and does not stray from its purpose. Sentences are complete, varied, and demonstrate correct grammatical conventions, such as accurate subject-verb agreement and pronoun usage. The rules of capitalization and punctuation are followed, and words are spelled correctly in almost all cases.

3 Points

The writer addresses the task specified in the writing prompt. The topic or main idea of the writing is generally supported through appropriate details, examples, reasons, or explanations, but some supporting ideas may be lacking or irrelevant. An organizational pattern is present, but the writer occasionally strays from it or confuses the order of ideas. The writer demonstrates a reasonable command of language, choosing appropriate words in most cases. The writing is reasonably complete and unified, but it may stray from its purpose from time to time. Sentences are complete and varied, although they may have simple structures and may contain errors in subject-verb agreement, pronoun usage, and other grammatical conventions. For the most part, capitalization, punctuation, and spelling are correct, though there may be some errors of each type throughout the paper.

2 Points

The writer addresses the task specified in the writing prompt but fails to develop it completely. The topic or main idea of the writing is supported with some appropriate details, examples, or reasons, but important supporting ideas are lacking and some of those given may be irrelevant. An organizational pattern has been attempted, but the writer often strays from it or confuses the order of ideas. The writer demonstrates a general command of language, but sometimes chooses inappropriate or imprecise words. The writing lacks completeness and unity, often straying from its purpose. Sentences, though generally complete, lack variety and contain some basic errors in subject-verb agreement, pronoun usage, and other grammatical conventions. Capitalization, punctuation, and spelling are generally correct, but there are a considerable number of errors of each type throughout the paper.

1 Point

The writer indicates limited understanding of the task specified in the writing prompt. The topic or main idea may be poorly developed or not explicitly stated. Few, if any, supporting ideas are offered, and unrelated information is included. The writing shows little or no evidence of an organizational plan or strategy. The writer demonstrates a weak command of language, and word choice is inappropriate, repetitive, or vague. The writing displays little or no sense of purpose. Sentences may be incomplete with many obvious errors in subject-verb agreement, pronoun usage, and other grammatical conventions, hindering the effectiveness of communication. There are frequent errors in capitalization, punctuation, and spelling.

Unscorable

The response is unrelated to the prompt, is simply a rewording of the prompt, or is plagiarized; OR the student refused to write, wrote illegibly, or wrote incomprehensibly; OR the response is related to the prompt, but does not carry enough information.

Name _____

Reading Test Form

Test: _____

1. Ⓐ Ⓑ Ⓒ Ⓓ
2. Ⓐ Ⓑ Ⓒ Ⓓ
3. Ⓐ Ⓑ Ⓒ Ⓓ
4. Ⓐ Ⓑ Ⓒ Ⓓ
5. Ⓐ Ⓑ Ⓒ Ⓓ
6. _____
_____
_____

Test: _____

1. Ⓐ Ⓑ Ⓒ Ⓓ
2. Ⓐ Ⓑ Ⓒ Ⓓ
3. Ⓐ Ⓑ Ⓒ Ⓓ
4. Ⓐ Ⓑ Ⓒ Ⓓ
5. Ⓐ Ⓑ Ⓒ Ⓓ
6. _____
_____
_____

Test: _____

1. Ⓐ Ⓑ Ⓒ Ⓓ
2. Ⓐ Ⓑ Ⓒ Ⓓ
3. Ⓐ Ⓑ Ⓒ Ⓓ
4. Ⓐ Ⓑ Ⓒ Ⓓ
5. Ⓐ Ⓑ Ⓒ Ⓓ
6. Ⓐ Ⓑ Ⓒ Ⓓ

Test: _____

1. Ⓐ Ⓑ Ⓒ Ⓓ
2. Ⓐ Ⓑ Ⓒ Ⓓ
3. Ⓐ Ⓑ Ⓒ Ⓓ
4. Ⓐ Ⓑ Ⓒ Ⓓ
5. Ⓐ Ⓑ Ⓒ Ⓓ
6. Ⓐ Ⓑ Ⓒ Ⓓ
7. Ⓐ Ⓑ Ⓒ Ⓓ
8. Ⓐ Ⓑ Ⓒ Ⓓ
9. Ⓐ Ⓑ Ⓒ Ⓓ
10. _____
_____
_____

Name _____

Writing Test Form

Test: _____

_____

_____

_____

_____

_____

_____

_____

_____

_____

_____

_____

_____

_____

_____

_____

_____

_____

_____

Idea Web

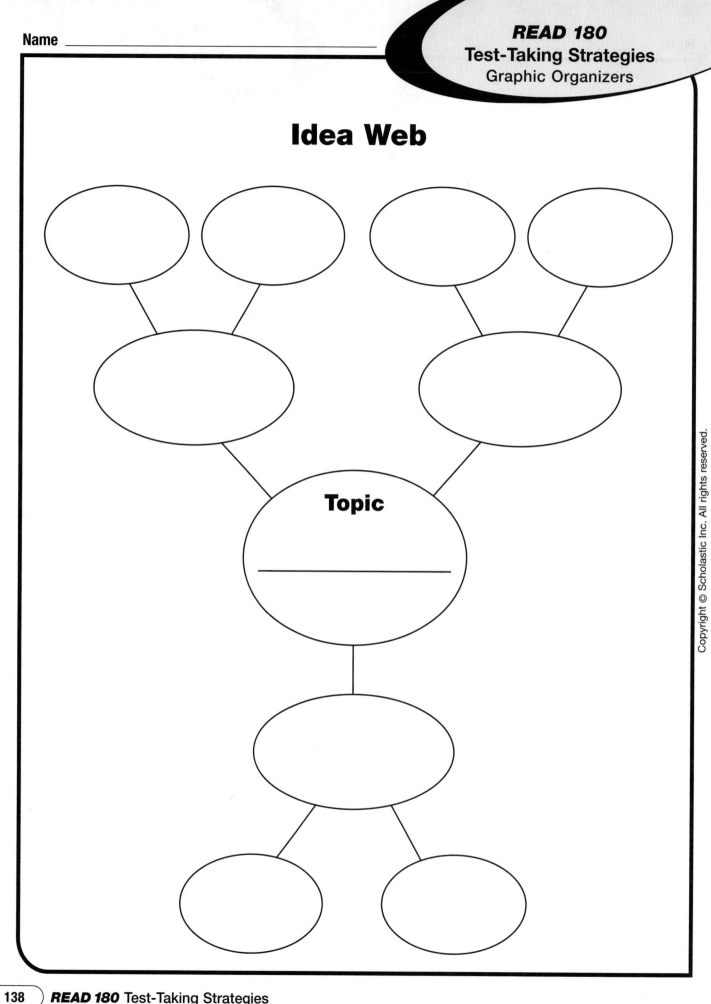

Topic

_____

Outline

I. **Introduction**

   A. Topic Sentence: _____

_____

_____

II. **Main Idea:** _____

   A. Supporting Detail: _____

   B. Supporting Detail: _____

III. **Main Idea:** _____

   A. Supporting Detail: _____

   B. Supporting Detail: _____

IV. **Main Idea:** _____

   A. Supporting Detail: _____

   B. Supporting Detail: _____

V. **Conclusion** _____

_____

_____

_____

Student Writing Self-Assessment

_____ **1.** Does your essay focus on the topic from the prompt?

_____ **2.** Did you write in complete sentences?

_____ **3.** Did you read over your essay and look for any mistakes in spelling and punctuation?

_____ **4.** Did you use transition words to connect ideas?

_____ **5.** Is your essay written in the 5-paragraph format?

_____ **6.** Did you use descriptive words when possible?

_____ **7.** Did you write neatly and legibly?

_____ **8.** Do your types of sentences vary?

_____ **9.** The questions and concerns I still have are _____

_____

_____ **10.** I still need help with _____

_____

Test Tips

To be successful on tests keep the following thoughts in mind:

✔ Stay in a good mood. A positive attitude can really help.

✔ Stay focused. Don't let others distract you during the test.

✔ Write neatly and legibly. You don't want to lose points because someone can't read your writing.

✔ Always review your answers before turning in the test. Make sure that your answers are in the correct order and that you have answered every question. Careless mistakes often cause wrong answers.

✔ Ask the teacher to seat you where you are comfortable. You should be aware of what distracts you. It is important to become responsible for your own needs.

✔ Come to school prepared for the test with sharpened pencils and clean erasers. You don't want little things like having to find a pencil or pen take time away from completing the test.

✔ Read all directions carefully. If you are unsure about the directions, ask your teacher for help. You should never be embarrassed to ask for help. It's better to make sure you understand the directions than to get an answer wrong.

✔ Don't worry about anyone else's work. A test is not a race.

✔ Attempt to answer all the questions. On many tests there is no harm in guessing.

✔ Don't spend too much time on any one question. You don't want time to slip away and then have to rush to finish.

✔ Don't second-guess yourself. Always stick with your first answer if you are unsure.

✔ Do your best. During a test, you can either choose to be your own best friend or your own worst enemy. It is easier to be your own best friend.

Brain Boosters

Our brains require certain treats to think properly. Below are ways to help make sure that you will be alert and ready for the test.

- Get a good night's sleep. It's important to get eight hours of sleep because your body needs time to rest.

- Make sure you take deep breaths. Your brain needs a lot of oxygen.

- Wake up with a positive attitude. Smile, put on your best outfit, and get to school on time.

- Eat a well-balanced breakfast. Your brain needs fuel, or nutrients, to function. Water and proteins are good nutrients for the brain. Stay away from high-sugar foods.

- Relax. Your brain knows when you feel stressed, worried, or anxious. Trust what you know. Do your very best.

Lesson Tracking

Lesson Title	Date Completed	Notes
1. *Making an Educated Guess*		
2. *Answering Fill-in-the-Blanks*		
3. *Restating the Question*		
4. *Previewing Questions*		
5. *Using Vocabulary Strategies*		
6. *Literal & Interpretive Questions*		
7. *Answering Proofreading Questions*		
8. *Using Cue Words: Compare, Cause/Effect*		
9. *Using Cue Words: Sequence, Fact/Opinion*		
10. *Using Cue Words: Literary Elements*		
11. *Using Text Evidence*		
12. *Justifying and Checking Your Answer*		
13. *Open-Ended Questions*		
14. *Using Test Time Effectively*		
15. *Identifying Narrative Prompts*		
16. *Identifying Expository Prompts*		
17. *Identifying Persuasive Prompts*		
18. *Restating the Prompt*		
19. *Generating Your Thoughts*		
20. *Creating an Outline*		
21. *Understanding Evaluation Criteria*		

Test Tracking

Practice Test	Date Completed	Score	Notes
Reading Test Level A, Test 1			
Reading Test Level A, Test 2			
Reading Test Level A, Test 3			
Reading Test Level A, Test 4			
Reading Test Level A, Test 5			
Reading Test Level A, Test 6			
Reading Test Level A, Test 7			
Reading Test Level B, Test 1			
Reading Test Level B, Test 2			
Reading Test Level B, Test 3			
Reading Test Level B, Test 4			
Reading Test Level B, Test 5			
Reading Test Level B, Test 6			
Reading Test Level B, Test 7			
Narrative Writing Test 1			
Narrative Writing Test 2			
Narrative Writing Test 3			
Expository Writing Test 1			
Expository Writing Test 2			
Expository Writing Test 3			
Persuasive Writing Test 1			
Persuasive Writing Test 2			
Persuasive Writing Test 3			

Name _____

Dear _____,

On _____, your child, _____, will be taking the _____ Test. This test measures the students' proficiency in reading and writing.

During the school year, we have worked on many test-taking strategies to help students become more confident when taking tests. Here are a few ways you can support these efforts at home:

- Make sure your child gets a good night's sleep.

- Help your child wake up in time to prepare for school.

- Provide a well-balanced breakfast.

- Give your child words of encouragement to help him or her to feel relaxed and comfortable about this test.

- Avoid unnecessary stress by ensuring that your child arrives on time and prepared.

Thank you for supporting these efforts!

Sincerely,

_____

Estimado/a Sr/a. _____,

El día_____, su hijo/a,_____, va a tomar la prueba
_____. Esta prueba o examen, mide la capacidad de leer y escribir de los estudiantes.

Durante el año escolar hemos enseñado muchas estrategias para ayudar a su hijo/a a tener más confianza al tomar cualquier prueba. A continuación, algunas maneras en las que usted puede ayudar con esta tarea:

- Asegúrese de que su hijo/a duerma lo suficiente.

- Ayúdelo/a a que se levante con tiempo para prepararse para la escuela.

- Déle un desayuno balanceado.

- Anímelo/a para que se sienta relajado y con una actitud positiva ante la prueba.

- Ayúdelo/a a evitar cualquier estrés innecesario asegurándose de que llegue a tiempo a la clase y esté bien preparado/a.

Muchas gracias por su cooperación.

Atentamente,

_____

Answer Key
Answers for Strategy Practice and Practice Tests

Lesson 1, p. 20.
1. D **2.** C **3.** C **4.** A **5.** C

Lesson 2, p. 23.
1. B **2.** A **3.** C **4.** C **5.** D

Lesson 3, p. 26.
1. Jasmine wants to raise money to buy a new stereo.
2. Her grandmother calls it a "private cafe" because Jasmine will cook burgers just like at the restaurant.
3. Jasmine needs Carla's help because her customers were upset that the burgers were taking too long to cook.
4. Jasmine convinces Carla to help her by promising to split the profit with her.
5. Jasmine and Carla decide to sell burgers again next year because they made money and had fun.
6. Possible answer: Based on her actions, Jasmine is considerate, thoughtful, and a good problem solver.

Lesson 4, p. 29.
1. What makes "the leaves hang trembling" is the passing wind. *Explain:* "But when the leaves hang trembling / The wind is passing thro'."
2. B *Explain:* "the trees bow down their heads"
3. The author is referring to the tops of the trees when using the words, "their heads." *Explain:* Possible answer: Just as our head is on the top of our bodies, the top of a tree can be described as its head.

Lesson 5, p. 32.
1. C *Explain:* "Because of this claim, American officials worried that bringing Texas into the United States might lead to war with Mexico."
2. In the first paragraph, the word rejected means "turned down." *Explain:* "The United States hesitated before making Texas a state." "Why was the United States so uneasy about making Texas a state?"
3. B *Explain:* "But the United States agreed to settle these arguments."

Lesson 6, p. 35.
1. Possible answer: From the way he interacts with Jorge, Dino can be described as outgoing and witty. *Explain:* interpretive
2. A *Explain:* literal
3. Possible answer: The Hammer learned how it feels to get embarrassed in front of his classmates. *Explain:* interpretive
4. B *Explain:* literal

Lesson 7, p. 37.
1. C *Explain:* grammar
2. A *Explain:* capitalization
3. B *Explain:* spelling
4. A *Explain:* punctuation

Lesson 8, p. 40.
1. The reason the moon appears to change shape is because we see the bright side of it from different directions over the course of a month. The passage says when the moon shines, it is reflecting light from the sun and that it does not really change shape. *Explain:* why
2. D *Explain:* compare
3. The sun's rotation period is different at its equator and at its poles. The rotation period of Earth is the same at every point on its surface. *Explain:* difference

Lesson 9, p. 43.
1. C *Explain:* opinion
2. His father had played the violin in a band on the plantation where he had been a slave. *Explain:* before, event
3. Opinion: "The rest of Joplin's life is a sad story." Fact: "His music was popular for a while, but it was not performed in concert halls during his lifetime." *Explain:* opinion, fact

(Continued on next page)

Answer Key, continued

Lesson 10, p. 46.

1. A *Explain:* lessons

2. "You are not faster than I am, but you found a way to slow me down." *Explain:* after, say

3. He wanted to marry Atalanta, and she did not want to marry. She would marry him only if he beat her in a race, and she was faster than he. *Explain:* problem, solve

Lesson 11, p. 49.

1. Possible answer: Keesha reacted with excitement. *Explain:* "Look! The lunch bag is leaping!"

2. D *Explain:* "Just then, it stopped moving, and a pink claw poked out."

3. Shawna and her family learned that they should pack their lunches in something safe rather than leave them out in the open. *Explain:* "'Well, next time we'll have to pack our lunches in a cooler,' Mom said."

Lesson 12, p. 52.

1. Scottish inventors added pedals to help turn the wheels. *Explain:* "Inventors in Scotland added pedals to help turn the wheels of the bicycle."

2. A *Explain:* "Finally, in 1880, inventors made a safer bicycle that was closer to the ground."

3. Mountain bikes ride smoothly on rocky ground because they are built with thick wheels and sturdy frames. *Explain:* "Mountain bikes have thick wheels and sturdy frames." "These features help make the ride smoother on rocky ground."

Lesson 13, p. 55.

1. The editorial says that Ms. Gonsalves does have enough experience. *Explain:* She has participated in the Beachview government as a member of the City Council, and she is president of the Chamber of Commerce.

2. It says Mayor de Carlo's style is confrontational and Ms. Gonsalves's style is more conciliatory, agreeable, and easygoing. *Explain:* It says Mayor de Carlo has been stubborn with Council members and alienated them, and that they are now unwilling to work with her or to support her programs. Ms. Gonsalves uses soothing words to appeal to friends and opponents.

3. Answers will vary. Those preferring Mayor de Carlo's plan may commend it because it is specific and includes a plan for funding, whereas Ms. Gonsalves has made no specific traffic proposals. Those preferring Ms. Gonsalves's plan may agree that more traffic lights would make congestion worse, and that she should seek the recommendations of experienced people.

Lesson 15, p. 59.

1. write an essay telling about a time

2. The response a test grader would expect to find is a story telling about a time when I was amazed by the power of nature. My story would have a beginning, a middle, and an end. It would focus on the things that made me aware of the power of natural forces.

3. write an essay telling about a day in your life

4. Answers will vary.

Lesson 16, p. 61.

1. explain how

2. The test grader would expect to find an explanation of how the object is used. The essay should focus on what the object looks like and how it is used. The essay should make clear the purpose or purposes for which the object is used.

3. explain how

4. Answers will vary.

Lesson 17, p. 63.

1. convince; opinion; support your choice

2. The response a test grader would expect is an essay to convince the class to choose a particular place for the field trip. The essay would begin by stating my opinion about a particular place that is the best place to go on the field trip. It would then offer several reasons supporting my opinion. The essay would close by summarizing my opinion and calling on the class to choose that place.

3. persuade school officials to agree with your position

4. Answers will vary.

(Continued on next page)

Lesson 18, p. 65.

1. A challenge that I faced was . . .
2. challenge, faced
3. A person who showed courage and stood up for what they believed in was . . .
4. person, showed courage, believed

Lesson 19, p. 67.

1. How debating will help me as an adult
- organize my thoughts better
- get information about important issues that I can talk about with my friends
- most jobs require some public speaking
- important to be able to express and support a point of view

2. Answers will vary.

Lesson 20, p. 69.

1. I want to visit the Grand Canyon
- one of America's great natural wonders
- can take a rafting trip on the Colorado River
- can hike the trails in the Canyon
- can see the effect of sunlight on the Canyon

Look for a well-organized outline on the topic from the prompt.
2. Answers will vary.

Lesson 21, p. 72.

Answers will vary. Sample answers are given.
1. Have you ever seen a rubber band before?
2. Rubber <u>stretches</u> when you pull on it.
3. There are many different ways rubber bands can be used.
4. Rubber bands come in all kinds of sizes and colors.
5. They are a <u>wonderful</u> invention.

Reading Practice Tests: Level A

Test 1, p. 74.
1. C **2.** A **3.** C **4.** A **5.** C
6. Possible answer: Jarod solves the problem by not letting the kids touch the bat and by calling a janitor.

Test 2, p. 76.
1. C **2.** D **3.** C **4.** B **5.** A **6.** C

Test 3, p. 78.
1. C **2.** B **3.** C **4.** A **5.** B
6. Possible answer: Ramon is enthusiastic, and he likes to learn about astronauts and space.

Test 4, p. 80.
1. B **2.** C **3.** C **4.** A **5.** D
6. Possible answer: The shells of eagles' eggs became thin and likely to crack because of chemicals in the bodies of small animals the eagles ate.

Test 5, p. 82.
1. A **2.** C **3.** C **4.** C **5.** B
6. Possible answer: The whorl pattern is made up of circles, but the arch pattern is made up of curves.

Test 6, p. 84.
1. B **2.** C **3.** C **4.** B **5.** A
6. Possible answer: The words in the poem that help set the tone of the "other girl's" point of view are *cracks*, *decay*, and *burden*.

Test 7, p. 86.
1. D **2.** A **3.** B **4.** A **5.** C
6. Possible answer: Soybeans make soy flour that is used in baby food, cereal, and baked goods.

(Continued on next page)

Answer Key, continued

Reading Practice Tests: Level B

Test 1, p. 88.

1. B **2.** A **3.** D **4.** D **5.** B **6.** C **7.** A **8.** B **9.** C
10. Tallulah received an email from one of the bank robbers by mistake and reported it to the police. The plainclothes detectives waited inside the bank and stopped the robbery.

Test 2, p. 92.

1. C **2.** D **3.** B **4.** D **5.** A **6.** C **7.** A **8.** B **9.** C
10. They go there to leave flowers, to honor the memory of Chun, and to thank him for saving their lives.

Test 3, p. 96.

1. C **2.** A **3.** D **4.** C **5.** A **6.** B

Test 4, p. 98.

1. C **2.** C **3.** A **4.** D **5.** B **6.** D **7.** C **8.** B **9.** B
10. Example: She was named Female Athlete of the Year in 1957, got a ticker-tape parade and the Medallion of the City from New York in the same year, was inducted into the International Tennis Hall of Fame in 1971, and entered the International Women's Sports Hall of Fame in 1980.

Test 5, p. 102.

1. C **2.** D **3.** A **4.** B **5.** D **6.** A **7.** C **8.** B **9.** B
10. Plans include building up the marshlands by using control gates, shoring up barrier islands in the gulf, and building a 20-foot wall in the city to seal off parts of downtown.

Test 6, p. 108.

1. B **2.** D **3.** A **4.** B **5.** C
6. The tourist concludes that this planet is populated by cars, and the "soft shapes" (humans) inside the cars are either the creatures' "guts" or their "brains."

Test 7, p. 110.

1. B **2.** D **3.** A **4.** B **5.** D **6.** C **7.** A **8.** C **9.** D
10. Native Americans gained confidence and pride from the protest, as well as greater respect for Indian culture and sovereignty.

Writing Practice Tests

See **Rubrics, pages 132–135.**